The Ptolemaic Kingdom

An Enthralling Guide to the Empire Where Ancient Egypt Met Greek Genius

© Copyright 2024 - All rights reserved.

The content contained within this book may not be reproduced, duplicated, or transmitted without direct written permission from the author or the publisher.

Under no circumstances will any blame or legal responsibility be held against the publisher, or author, for any damages, reparation, or monetary loss due to the information contained within this book, either directly or indirectly.

Legal Notice:

This book is copyright protected. It is only for personal use. You cannot amend, distribute, sell, use, quote, or paraphrase any part, or the content within this book, without the consent of the author or publisher.

Disclaimer Notice:

Please note the information contained within this document is for educational and entertainment purposes only. All effort has been executed to present accurate, up-to-date, reliable, and complete information. No warranties of any kind are declared or implied. Readers acknowledge that the author is not engaging in the rendering of legal, financial, medical, or professional advice. The content within this book has been derived from various sources. Please consult a licensed professional before attempting any techniques outlined in this book.

By reading this document, the reader agrees that under no circumstances is the author responsible for any losses, direct or indirect, that are incurred as a result of the use of the information contained within this document, including, but not limited to, errors, omissions, or inaccuracies.

Free limited time bonus

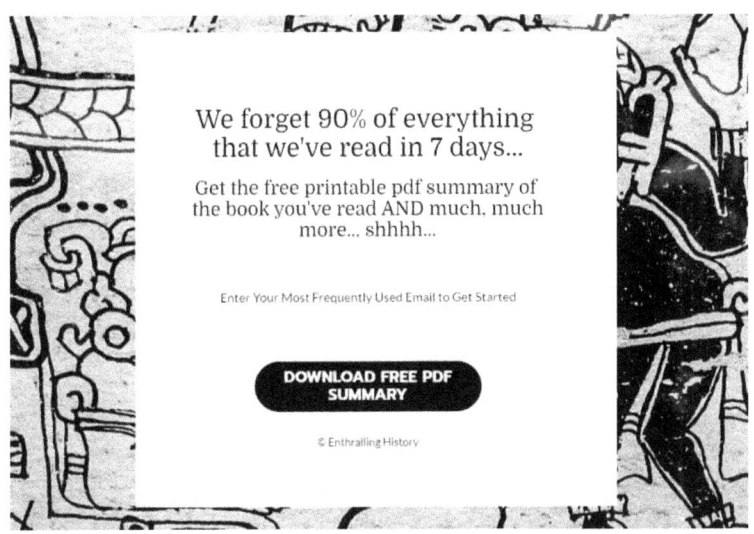

Stop for a moment. We have a free bonus set up for you. The problem is this: we forget 90% of everything that we read after 7 days. Crazy fact, right? Here's the solution: we've created a printable, 1-page pdf summary for this book that you're reading now. All you have to do to get your free pdf summary is to go to the following website: https://livetolearn.lpages.co/enthrallinghistory/

Or, Scan the QR code!

Once you do, it will be intuitive. Enjoy, and thank you!

Table of Contents

INTRODUCTION 1
CHAPTER 1: BIRTH OF A DYNASTY: THE RISE OF THE
PTOLEMIES 3
CHAPTER 2: ALEXANDRIA, THE JEWEL OF THE
MEDITERRANEAN 20
CHAPTER 3: THE FIRST FIVE PTOLEMAIC RULERS 29
CHAPTER 4: CULTURAL FUSION: GREEK INFLUENCE ON
EGYPTIAN SOCIETY 46
CHAPTER 5: THE GREAT LIBRARY OF ALEXANDRIA 55
CHAPTER 6: PTOLEMAIC ECONOMY 61
CHAPTER 7: THE PTOLEMAIC WARS AND STRATEGIES FOR
SURVIVAL 71
CHAPTER 8: DECLINE AND FALL OF PTOLEMAIC RULE 84
CHAPTER 9: LEGACY OF THE PTOLEMAIC KINGDOM
BEYOND EGYPT 102
CONCLUSION 107
HERE'S ANOTHER BOOK BY ENTHRALLING HISTORY THAT
YOU MIGHT LIKE 109
FREE LIMITED TIME BONUS 110
BIBLIOGRAPHY 111
IMAGE SOURCES 114

Introduction

Roaring cheers rang out as Alexander the Great marched into Egypt in 332 BCE. The Egyptians pragmatically hailed him as their savior from the oppressive Persians. Undoubtedly, the Egyptians had been weighing their options as Alexander's army approached Egypt.

"Did you hear what Alexander did in Tyre because they resisted for six months? He crucified the men!"

Everyone shuddered. "He smashed Gaza's walls down! Wasn't that supposed to be impossible?"

"That coward, King Darius, ran off the battlefield when he met Alexander's army! He left his men behind. He even left the royal women behind!"

"It's weird that the Persians take their women to war. Now Alexander has the queen, her two daughters, and the queen mother!"

"They say he's treating them well."

The Egyptians nodded. "It's no use resisting. We're better off welcoming him. After all, we share a common enemy."

And thus, the Egyptians danced, sang, and threw flowers as Alexander arrived. His trusted general, Ptolemy, rode at his side. A decade later, Ptolemy became Egypt's first Macedonian pharaoh, the mastermind of an exciting fusion of Hellenistic and Egyptian culture. His dynasty lasted three centuries, ending when Egypt's pharaoh, Cleopatra VII, committed suicide.

What came in between? The Ptolemaic Kingdom brought spectacular strides in science, mathematics, art, architecture, and economics. The glistening city of Alexandria beckoned scholars and artists to its intellectual and creative hub. Yet, the Ptolemaic Kingdom also featured ruinous family feuds, unbridled ambition, horrendous wars, and epic rebellions.

This book dives into the stories of the Ptolemaic pharaohs and how this unique kingdom shaped history, bridging the legacies of two ancient civilizations. What unexpected event led to Ptolemy's takeover of Egypt? How did he and his successors merge Greek and Egyptian cultural elements like art, architecture, and religion? For instance, why did the Ptolemaic pharaohs marry their sisters? Was that an Egyptian or Macedonian thing?

Did the Alexandrian Library really have a half million scrolls? Which Ptolemaic pharaoh ordered the translation of the Jewish Torah into Greek, and why? Who figured out that the Earth travels around the sun each year and rotates on its axis once a day? What genius who studied at the Library of Alexandria discovered pi (π), the law of the lever, and the compound pully?

The Ptolemaic Kingdom had few dull moments. This book unlocks the empire-building, scientific breakthroughs, and royal family drama. Two rich cultures came together, yet each kept their distinctive identities. More than anything, it is a story of passionate people and power struggles. This book brings their trials and triumphs to life as the Ptolemaic dynasty's story unfolds.

What's the point of reading history? Aside from being fascinating and fun, knowing the past helps us understand our present. History helps us recognize the catalysts for change, both good and bad. We especially see the intrinsic role of leadership. Wise rulers lead their country into prosperity, progress, and peace. Inept leaders can drag their country into desperate straits. The Ptolemaic Kingdom had both. Let's unpack how it all played out.

Chapter 1: Birth of a Dynasty: The Rise of the Ptolemies

"Ptolemy! Come quickly!"

In the dead of night, Ptolemy awakened to someone pounding on his door. It was Lysimachus. Like Ptolemy, he was an officer under Alexander and one of his seven bodyguards.

"It's Alexander! He's getting worse!"

Ptolemy frowned. Alexander had fallen ill a week earlier, shortly after a flock of ravens fell from the sky, dying at his feet. Alexander had fever, chills, excessive thirst, and abdominal pain.

"Is the doctor there? What's happening?"

"Yes, his doctor is there, and they've called in some specialists from Babylon. He can barely speak or sit up. When he does say something, it makes no sense. He's delirious!"

"Let's go!" Ptolemy threw on his cape and grabbed his sword. "He needs his friends there!"

They hurried to Alexander's quarters, where the doctors huddled. Alexander's first wife, Roxanne, sat at the bedside, her belly swollen with his only child. The doctors' best efforts were hopeless. Struggling to breathe, Alexander became increasingly weaker.[i] Four days later, he died

---

[i] J. S. Marr and C. H. Calisher, "Alexander the Great and West Nile Virus Encephalitis," *Emerging Infectious Diseases*, 9, no. 12 (December 2003): 599-603, https://doi: 10.3201/eid0912.030288. PMID: 14725285; PMCID: PMC3034319.

at age thirty-two, leaving a vast empire that spread over three continents.

"I'm burying him in Egypt!" Ptolemy declared. "That's where he wanted to be buried. I was with him when the priest at Memphis crowned him the new pharaoh. I heard the oracle at the Siwa Oasis declare him the son of Egypt's high god Amun! Alexander wanted to be buried in the land of his heavenly father."

What would happen to Alexander's empire? Who was Ptolemy I Soter, and what did he and his fellow officers do after Alexander died? What power plays in the Middle East, Egypt, Greece, and Macedonia led up to this point? To answer these questions, we have to go back.

Ancient Middle East map [1]

How did two major Middle Eastern shakedowns affect everything?

In 612 BCE, Babylon joined a massive coalition force to destroy the Neo-Assyrian Empire. The Assyrians had terrorized the Middle East for three hundred years. The surviving Assyrian royals escaped to Syria, hoping to regroup and make a comeback. They desperately messaged Pharoah Necho of Egypt, their only remaining ally. Necho mustered his forces and marched north.

King Josiah of Judah barred Necho's way, refusing passage through his country. In Megiddo, Necho killed Josiah and defeated the Judean army. But the delay doomed the Assyrians and Egyptians. Eager to utterly destroy the Assyrians, the Babylonians had surrounded Carchemish. Necho found Nebuchadnezzar II, Babylon's crown prince, waiting for him.

In the brutal 605 BCE Battle of Carchemish, the Babylonians wiped out the Egyptian army and the Assyrian nobility. Assyria never recovered, and Egypt went into a tailspin. Up to this point, Egypt had controlled much of the coastland between Egypt and Syria. Necho lost it all to the Babylonians and never got it back, except for Gaza, the ancient Philistine city. Egypt lost control of its lucrative trade routes, especially with Phoenicia. Economically and militarily weakened, Egypt limped along for 130 years until it fell prey to Persia, as foretold by the Jewish prophet Ezekiel:

> "For so said the Lord God: The sword of the king of Babylon will come upon you. With the swords of the mighty, I shall cause your multitude to fall, all of them the strong of the nations, and they will plunder the pride of Egypt, and all its multitude will be destroyed."[i]

Nebuchadnezzar II swept Judah, the Sinai Peninsula, Syria, southern Turkey, and ancient Iraq into the Neo-Babylonian Empire. Yet, his descendants turned out to be inept rulers. Decades later, Cyrus the Great united the Medes and Persians (today's Iran), and their joint forces conquered Central Asia and the entire Babylonian Empire by 539 BCE.

What was happening in Egypt before Alexander arrived?

Cyrus the Great planned to invade Egypt, but first, he wanted to subdue the troublesome nomadic tribes northeast of Persia. That proved a fatal move. Queen Tomyris of the Massagetae sliced off his head in 530 BCE. Five years later, Cyrus's son, Cambyses, attacked Egypt. The Egyptians fought fiercely to defend their land with archers, catapults, and

---

[i] *The Complete Tanakh: The Jewish Bible with a Modern English Translation and Rashi's Commentary.* https://www.chabad.org/library/bible_cdo/aid/63255/jewish/The-Bible-with-Rashi.htm, Nevi'im, Yechezkel (Ezekiel) 32:11-12.

chariots. Yet, Phanes of Halicarnassus, once a Greek mercenary for Egypt, defected to the Persians' side. He suggested an ingenious and unusual battle strategy: cats!

The Egyptian war goddess was Bastet, who featured a woman's body and a cat's head. The Egyptians considered cats sacred animals, and killing a cat brought the death penalty. Phanes instructed the Persians, "This is how you can unhinge the Egyptians—paint Bastet's portrait on your shields. Round up hundreds of cats and let them go on your frontlines. They won't want to shoot at you for fear of harming a cat or hitting Bastet's image."

As they gathered at the battlefield, the Egyptians stared in horror. What could they do? They didn't dare incur Bastet's wrath. Suddenly, the Egyptians turned and ran away.[i] Egypt unhappily became part of the Persian-Achaemenid Empire in 525 BCE. For the first time in history, foreigners ruled Egypt. The Egyptians spent the next two centuries trying to break free from Persia. The Persians cruelly repressed any rebellion as the Egyptians seethed.

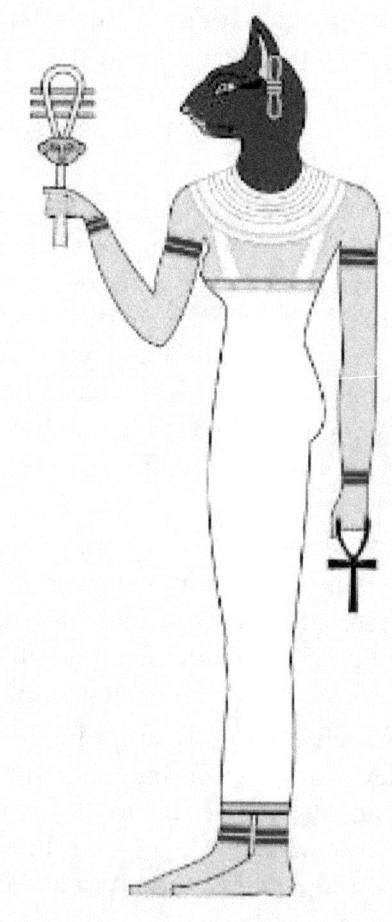

Bastet, Egyptian goddess of war[2]

---

[i] Polyaenus, *Stratagems: Book Seven*, trans. R. Shepherd, 1793, http://www.attalus.org/translate/polyaenus7.html.

Persia's Cambyses II captures Pharaoh Psamtik III.[3]

What was the situation in Greece and Macedonia?

In ancient times, Greece was never a unified country. Instead, it had multiple city-states with independent governments. On rare occasions, they united to fight the Persians. However, most of the time, the Greek city-states fought each other. Macedonia was a large but poor Greek kingdom that covered modern-day North Macedonia, part of today's northern Greece, and bits of Albania, Serbia, Bulgaria, and Kosovo. It had never been a significant player in the ancient world and was in peril of being swallowed up by its neighbors. When Philip II became king, everything changed.

Philip spent his teen years as a hostage in the Greek city-state of Thebes, where he learned the Theban art of war. He returned to Macedonia with an extraordinarily ambitious goal. He would transform Macedonia into the world's premier fighting machine. Philip even developed his own weapon, a spear called a sarissa that was three times longer than a man.

Among his soldiers was a young man named Ptolemy. He was older than Philip's son Alexander, but the two of them had studied together under Aristotle. Philip had hired the renowned philosopher to tutor his son and the sons of other nobility. Ptolemy was officially the son of a nobleman named Lagos, yet rumors swirled that he was Philip's illegitimate son and Alexander's half-brother. That's doubtful because, unlike the other Greeks, the Macedonian kings could have more than one wife. Philip had four wives from foreign royal families. He also had three lesser wives or concubines and a series of male lovers, usually his bodyguards.

Macedonian army with sarissas⁴

With a well-trained army and his bristling sarissas, Philip set out to build his empire. He started with the lands surrounding Macedonia. Once he accomplished this, Philip left his sixteen-year-old son Alexander as regent of Macedonia while he marched south to conquer central Greece. A few years later, Philip and Alexander overpowered all southern Greece except Sparta. Macedonia and most of Greece formed the League of Corinth in 337 BCE, which was determined to bring Persia to its knees.

And then, it all came crashing down. Just before marching into Asia, Philip hosted a wedding for his daughter. Everyone was horrified when his bodyguard, a jilted lover, suddenly shoved a dagger into Philip's side. With Philip's blood pooling in the banquet hall, the Macedonian generals crowned Alexander their new king.

As soon as they heard, Athens and Thebes pulled out of the League of Corinth, followed swiftly by several other Greek cities. Alexander spent the next year thrashing the Greeks until they got back on board. Then, in 334 BCE, Alexander, Ptolemy, and 40,000 soldiers crossed the Dardanelles Strait into Asia.

Alexander and Ptolemy in Asia

The Persian navy was superior to Alexander's, so he needed to change that. He successfully attacked Miletus and Halicarnassus, Persia's most important naval ports (in today's western Turkey). Without the ports, the Persian navy couldn't get supplies and reinforcements. Alexander left Ptolemy and three thousand troops to finish mopping up in Halicarnassus. When the unsuspecting Persian warships sailed into their homeport, Ptolemy's men pounced on them, commandeering the ships for the Greek navy.

Ptolemy caught up with Alexander just before the crucial Battle of Issus. They were marching down the Mediterranean coast, near the border of Anatolia (Turkey) and Syria, when suddenly they were ambushed. Persia's King Darius launched a surprise attack at their rear. He trapped Alexander's army between the sea and the mountains. However, Alexander's well-trained and highly disciplined army immediately fell into formation.

Ptolemy was on the left flank with General Parmenion and the cavalry from Thessalonia and Thrace. Alexander and his Macedonian cavalry were on the right flank with the Bulgarian javelin throwers. The infantry, with their eighteen-foot-long sarissas, held the middle. The swiftly flowing Pinarus River separated the Greeks from the Persians.

King Darius panicking on the battlefield[5]

The Persian cavalry galloped across the river, crashing into the Macedonian left side as Parmenion and Ptolemy desperately fended them off. Alexander raced his Macedonian cavalry over the river toward the Persian foot soldiers. Meanwhile, the Macedonian infantry tried to cross but floundered in the swiftly flowing river. Their shields and unwieldy sarissas weighed them down. The Persian archers shot volleys of arrows toward the helpless men in the river, darkening the sky.

When Alexander realized his infantry was in peril, he charged toward the Persians' middle section to draw off the archers. King Darius's chariot was in the center section. When he saw Alexander ferociously racing in his direction, Darius froze, petrified with fear. Then, he whipped his horses around and fled the battlefield, leaving his men behind. Eventually, the Persians realized their king had abandoned the battle. They looked at each other, shrugged, and ran after him.

The second time Alexander and Ptolemy faced off against Darius was in the pivotal Battle of Gaugamela in today's northern Iraq. This time, Darius was better prepared. His army was twice the size of Alexander's, and he had war elephants and two hundred chariots with razor-sharp scythes that could cut a man's leg in half protruding from their wheel hubs. The Macedonians and Greeks had not fought against elephants or scythed chariots before.

Once again, Alexander stationed his cavalry forces on each end, with his infantry in the middle. Ptolemy and Parmenion were on the left flank again. After several skirmishes, Alexander's infantry pretended to retreat. The

Pompeii mosaic of Alexander at the Battle of Issus⁶

Persian cavalry chased them, leaving a gap in the Persian lines. Instantly, Alexander charged through the gap, his horses mowing down the Persian infantry. Darius sent his scythed chariots out, but the Bulgarian javelin-throwers picked off the charioteers as the Greek foot soldiers nimbly dodged the scythes. Darius was so unnerved that he forgot to deploy his elephants. Instead, shaking in horror, he raced off the battlefield again.

Alexander suddenly realized that the Persian cavalry was mowing down his left flank. He rushed over to save Parmenion, Ptolemy, and their cavalry. It was a brutal fight in which sixty Macedonian horsemen died. Eventually, the Persians realized their king had fled the field and abandoned the battle, to the Greeks' relief. Alexander had scored two victories over the Persians. However, King Darius was still out there.

Darius fled east, hoping to regroup and assemble another army. But betrayal cut his plans short. Bessus, his satrap (governor) of Bactria, murdered him, announcing himself as Persia's new king. Alexander gave Darius a royal burial, then sent Ptolemy east to hunt Bessus down. The Bactrians did not want to fight Alexander, so they left Bessus at the side of the road, chained to a stake. Ptolemy placed an iron collar with a chain around Bessus's neck and dragged him naked back to Alexander. Darius's brother, Oxathres, cut off Bessus's nose and ears, then tied him to a cross where archers shot arrows at him until he died.[i]

Alexander marched on to Persepolis, the ceremonial capital of the Persian Empire. Ptolemy's mistress, Thais, who was from Athens, was in Persepolis at the time. The Athenians held a bitter grudge against the former Persian king Xerxes. A half-century earlier, he had burned their beautiful city and destroyed the ancient temples. In Persepolis, the Macedonians and Greeks enjoyed a grand banquet, and everyone was drunk. Suddenly, Thais jumped up and made a speech:

> "Sitting here at this luxurious dinner brings me immense pleasure after all the hardships of wandering around Asia. Do you know what would make it even sweeter? Let's set fire to Xerxes's palace! That disgraceful man burned Athens down! He committed sacrilege against our great temples. I'll throw the first torch myself! People should know that the women who follow Alexander have gotten revenge for the atrocities the Persians did to Greece."[ii]

---

[i] Arrian, "Alexander the Great," in *The Anabasis and the Indica*, trans. Martin Hammond (Oxford University Press, 2013).

[ii] Diodorus, Siculus, *Library of History, Volume VIII*, trans. C. Bradford Welles (Harvard University Press, 1963).

The Greeks leaped up, cheering loudly. Alexander arose from his couch. Holding up a torch, Alexander beckoned to the female musicians to follow him, playing their flutes and singing. With Thais leading the way, Alexander and all the officers traipsed outside to Xerxes's palace, where Thais hurled the first torch. Everyone else threw their torches, and flames consumed the palace.

Alexander was eager to march east to the Ganges River in India, the "end of the world." Yet, he and his men had been conquering Asia for four years, and his soldiers were tired and homesick. General Parmenion's son Philotas led a conspiracy to assassinate Alexander. When he discovered the plot, Alexander executed Philotas and then selected seven trusted friends as his bodyguards. Ptolemy was one of the seven.

They reached the Persian Empire's eastern boundary, the Jaxartes River, and crossed over. Alexander's weary men forged on, climbing the 3,500-foot Khyber Pass over the Hindu Kush mountains and descending into the Indian subcontinent. Ptolemy commanded one-third of Alexander's forces on this expedition. A poisoned arrow struck Ptolemy at the Indus River, and Alexander used herbs to draw out the poison.

But Alexander never made it to the Ganges. His men mutinied, refusing to go one step further east. Enough was enough! Alexander had no choice but to return with his men to Persia.

In 324 BCE, he threw a huge wedding celebration in Susa. Ninety Persian princesses married the Greek and Macedonian nobles. It was a fusion of East and West. Alexander married King Darius's daughter, Stateira, and Parysatis, the daughter of Artaxerxes III, an earlier king. He gave the Persian princess Artakama to be Ptolemy's bride. Alexander also reunited with his first wife, Roxana, the daughter of a Sogdian chieftain, who soon became pregnant.

What happened when Alexander the Great unexpectedly died?

Alexander never saw Roxana's child. His sudden death, as we described earlier, cast everything into confusion. Who would replace Alexander? Roxana was due to give birth in three months. Alexander had a half-brother named Arrhidaeus, but he was cognitively challenged. Alexander's generals met to hash out a plan.

General Perdiccas held up Alexander's ring. "Alexander gave this to me on his deathbed. He meant for me to serve as regent for Arrhidaeus and Roxana's son. Arrhidaeus is Alexander's only living brother."

"We don't know if Roxana's baby is a boy or girl!" the other generals grumbled. "Even if it's a boy, he won't be able to rule on his own for years. And we all know Arrhidaeus isn't up to the task. If you're their regent, you're the de facto emperor."

"Why don't we wait to decide until Roxana gives birth?" one general suggested.

Ptolemy growled, "Look here! Roxana's child shouldn't even factor into our decision. She's not Macedonian or Greek. She's a Sogdian war captive. Do we want the conquered ruling the conquerors?"

"You have a point," General Meleager murmured. "Maybe we should give Arrhidaeus a chance."

"He hasn't the intellect! Does he even want to be the emperor?" the generals protested. However, a roar of approval from the soldiers filtering into the room drowned them out.

"Bring Arrhidaeus in!"

Meleager went out to get Arrhidaeus, but the overwhelmed young man took one look at the generals and fled. One of the soldiers gently persuaded him to return. The soldiers flung Alexander's royal cape over his trembling shoulders and handed him Alexander's crown.

Tears streaming down his face, Arrhidaeus protested. "I am not worthy. Someone more qualified should wear it!"

The next day, the generals met again. They agreed to have two kings: Roxana's child (if a boy) and Arrhidaeus. Perdiccas, Meleager, and Arrhidaeus would form a triumvirate, ruling together. However, Perdiccas's soldiers grumbled. "Alexander chose Perdiccas as his regent! Why is Meleager inserting himself?"

The soldiers murdered Meleager, sending everyone back to the drawing board.

Ptolemy cleared his throat. "I suggest doing away with the idea of one huge kingdom. We should divide the empire into loosely united states. Instead of a king over the empire, we'll have a council representing all the states."

Everyone looked blankly at Ptolemy. Yes, they were in unprecedented times, but Ptolemy's proposal was such a radical break from tradition that they couldn't wrap their heads around it. Finally, they agreed to the Partition of Babylon. Arrhidaeus would be king. They arranged for him to marry his niece, Eurydice. If Roxana's child were a boy, he would be a joint king. They would follow Alexander's wishes for Perdiccas to be regent, and he would also command the empire's army.

Third century BCE bust of Ptolemy I

The generals followed Ptolemy's advice about dividing the empire among themselves. Technically, they answered to the dual kings, but each took a large swathe of land to rule. Macedon, Illyria, and Greece went to Antipater, who had already ruled them as Alexander's regent for the past decade. One-eyed Antigonus took the rest of the provinces in Anatolia (Turkey). Ptolemy took Egypt, Arabia, and Libya. Syria went to Laomedon, and Arcesilaus got Mesopotamia (ancient Iraq). The eastern provinces continued under the leadership of the Asian leaders already ruling them.

Perdiccas ordered Alexander's body be sent back to Macedonia for burial in his family necropolis. Nevertheless, Ptolemy was determined to bury Alexander in Egypt. The mourners put the body in a casket full of honey. As they passed through Damascus, Syria, on the way to Macedonia, Ptolemy stole Alexander's body! He hauled the casket to Egypt. At first, he placed Alexander in a tomb in Memphis. Later, he moved the casket to the new city of Alexandria. Three hundred years later, Octavian (Caesar Augustus) began the tradition of Roman emperors visiting Alexander's burial site to pay their respects.

Ptolemy insisted he was honoring Alexander's wishes, and he probably was, at least partially. (Alexander had said he wanted to be buried at the Siwa Oasis, not Memphis or Alexandria.) Nevertheless, the Macedonian custom was for the new king to bury the one who just died. His rivals were sure that Ptolemy was openly challenging Perdiccas for the empire's throne. Was he? Ptolemy's role in the Wars of the Diadochi sheds some light on that question. But first, let's look at his family situation.

Ptolemy's First Wives

One of Ptolemy's first steps after Alexander's death was rearranging his private life. Athenaeus of Naucratis said that Ptolemy married his mistress, Thais, who had instigated the palace burning in Persepolis. There may have been some rivalry between Ptolemy and Alexander regarding the young woman. Athenaeus said that Alexander liked having Thais around. However, he might have meant that he found her amusing, not that they were sexually involved. Thais was known for being witty and fun.

At any rate, Ptolemy and Thais had three children together. Yet, his oldest son, Lagus, did not inherit his father's throne, and Ptolemy did not make Thais his queen. She had been a hetaira: an entertainer and conversationalist at the men's banquets who also provided sexual services. However, Ptolemy did arrange a wedding for their daughter Eirene to King Eunostos of the city-state of Soloi on the island of Cyprus.

As mentioned, Ptolemy had married the Persian princess Artakama in the mass wedding orchestrated by Alexander shortly before his death.

Artakama was the great-granddaughter of Artaxerxes II, king of the Persian Empire. However, she disappeared from history after Alexander's death. Many Greek officers who married Persian princesses in the mass wedding at Susa divorced them when Alexander died. Artakama's lineage of Persian royalty would have been awkward for Ptolemy since he wanted people to see him as their savior from harsh Persian rule.

Ptolemy I, Egypt's first Greek pharaoh⁹

Ptolemy and the Wars of the Diadochi

Diadochi means "successors," and these wars between Alexander's officers rocked his former empire for decades. The generals had divided the empire, but the one-time comrades-in-arms were now at each other's throats. Roxana gave birth to a son, Alexander IV, three months after Alexander died. To eliminate any competition, she poisoned

Alexander's two Persian wives. General Perdiccas helped her dispose of the bodies in a well.[i]

The uneasy truce between Alexander's successors quickly crumbled. Perdiccas married Antipater's daughter Nicaea but then discovered that the husband of Alexander's sister Cleopatra had died. She was back on the marriage market. If he married her, he could be king of Macedonia. He messaged Cleopatra with a proposal, telling her he intended to divorce Nicaea. When Antipater found out, he was livid. Cleopatra rejected his offer, but the damage was done.

Ptolemy, Antipater, and Antigonus formed a rebel force. Meanwhile, Perdiccas vowed revenge against Ptolemy for stealing Alexander's body. In the First War of the Diadochi (322-321 BCE), Perdiccas invaded Egypt.

When he reached the easternmost branch of the Nile near Pelusium, he realized Ptolemy had a large garrison stationed there. He marched north along the Nile until he reached a shallow ford across from Avaris. Perdiccas tried to cross the Nile with his elite infantry and war elephants. However, the Ptolemaic forces stopped him. Perdiccas turned south and marched toward Memphis. The Nile's current here was strong, but his strategy was to line his elephants across the river, forming an elephant dam to slow the river's force. He also lined his cavalry across the Nile downstream to rescue any of his infantry that lost their footing while wading across. This plan worked initially, and part of his army crossed to an island in the middle of the Nile.

But then, disaster struck. The elephants' feet got stuck in the mud, and they couldn't withstand the Nile's strong current. The elephant dam began falling apart, and the river grew too swift for more soldiers to cross. Worse, the soldiers on the island couldn't get back to shore. Over two thousand men drowned or were devoured by crocodiles trying to get off the island.

It was all over for Perdiccas. He had lost the confidence of his army, what was left of it. That night, three of his officers murdered him, and his army defected to Ptolemy.

The officers wanted Ptolemy to be the next regent of the empire, but he refused. He thought it was safer to maintain control of his chunk of

---

[i] Plutarch, *The Life of Alexander the Great*, trans. John Dryden (Modern Library Paperback Edition, 2004).

the empire than to take a gamble on ruling the whole thing.[1]

With Perdiccas dead, who would be regent? The generals made Antipater the new regent and co-ruler with Arrhidaeus. Antipater took King Arrhidaeus, Queen Eurydice, Roxana, and baby Alexander IV back to Macedonia for their safety. At this point, Ptolemy cemented his alliance with Antipater by marrying his daughter, Eurydice (not Arrhidaeus's wife). They had four or five children together. In 317 BCE, Ptolemy married Eurydice's lady-in-waiting and cousin, Berenice. Her oldest son with Ptolemy was Ptolemy II Philadelphus.

Antipater's death in 319 BCE caused a new crisis in the empire. Just before he died, he appointed another of Alexander's generals, Polyperchon, as his successor. Hardly anyone was pleased with this arrangement, especially Antipater's son Cassander, who had expected to be the next regent. In the Second War of the Diadochi (318-316 BCE), Ptolemy and Antigonus supported Cassander in ejecting Polyperchon and making Arrhidaeus the only king, with Queen Eurydice as his de facto regent.

Polyperchon scooped up Roxana and her four-year-old son Alexander IV and took them to Epirus. He allied with Alexander the Great's mother, Olympias, to fight Arrhidaeus and Eurydice. This proved successful because the Macedonian military refused to fight the mother of Alexander. Meanwhile, Cassander, Ptolemy, and Antigonus were too late to save Alexander's brother. Arrhidaeus and Eurydice died under Olympias's orders.

When Cassander arrived in Macedonia, he had no qualms about killing Olympias. He locked Roxana and her son Alexander in a tower in Macedonia, where they languished for years.

Ptolemy returned to Egypt to protect his kingdom, while Polyperchon fled to southern Greece, where he controlled Corinth and much of the Peloponnese Peninsula.

Antigonus ended up controlling virtually all western and central Asian—an enormous swathe of territory—but Ptolemy wanted Syria, Judea, and Cyprus. They would serve as buffer zones for Egypt and would bring lucrative trade. The Third War of the Diadochi (315-311 BCE) began when Ptolemy allied with another of Alexander's generals, Seleucus, to

---

[1] Diodorus, *Library of History*, Volume IX.

fight Antigonus.

Ptolemy invaded Syria; however, Antigonus took it back. Then, word arrived that Cassander had poisoned the boy-king, Alexander IV. Ptolemy was now fully Egypt's ruler, and it was no longer part of an empire.

Chapter 2: Alexandria, the Jewel of the Mediterranean

In 332 BCE, following his conquest of Gaza, Alexander the Great crossed the Sinai Desert with his 40,000 troops. After endless miles of blistering sand and jagged mountains, the landscape gradually turned lush and green. They soon arrived in Pelusium on the eastern edge of the Nile Delta.

Alexander's navy had sailed north from Phoenicia and was waiting for him in Pelusium's harbor. The Persian governor Mazaces (or Mazaus) graciously welcomed Alexander. He knew Alexander's arrival meant a new era in Egypt. King Darius had disgracefully run away from the Battle of Issus, at which the previous governor of Egypt had died, and Mazaces had only been in charge for a few months. Alexander had conquered or accepted the willing surrender of the coastal cities of Syria and Phoenicia. Mazaces hoped being friendly to Alexander would bring him a prominent position in the new empire, and it did.

After leaving an army unit in Pelusium, Alexander led his troops along the Nile to Memphis, Egypt's capital. Meanwhile, his navy sailed up the Nile to meet him there. The Egyptians looked on approvingly as he offered sacrifices to the primary Egyptian gods. Everyone enjoyed the show when Alexander's Greek artists put on a music and gymnastics performance.

From Memphis, Alexander sailed north with his fleet, following the westernmost branch of the Nile back to the Mediterranean. This part of the seacoast had an isthmus with the sea on one side and a lake on the other. Alexander sailed around the lake, where Bedouins lived in their tents. The more Alexander saw of the area, the more excited he got.

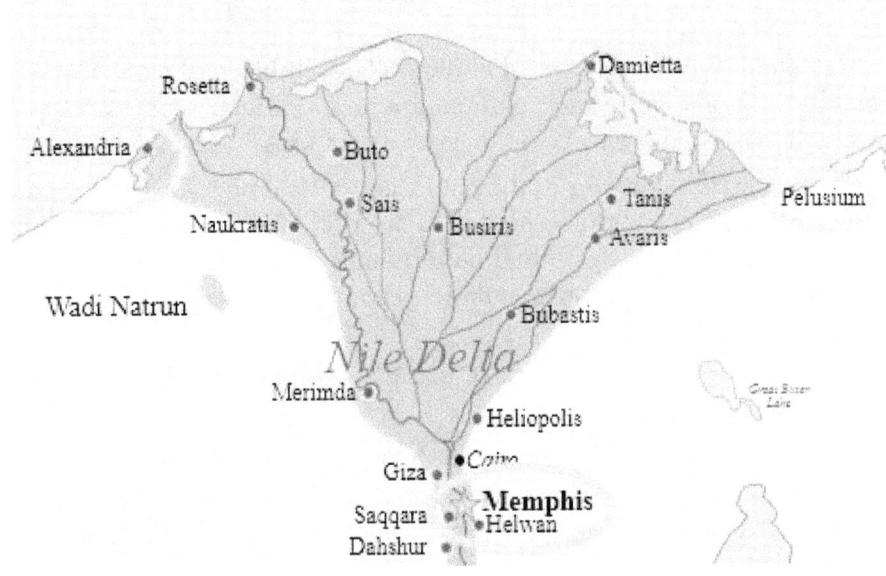

Alexandria and the Nile Delta

"Ptolemy! This isthmus would make a great area for a city! It's perfect for trade around the Mediterranean. We'll build a port where the Nile empties into the sea."

Ptolemy nodded. "It's not far from Greece. I can imagine a lot of trade back and forth."

"That's right! Egypt produces more than enough grain. We'll ship it to Greece from here." Alexander dipped his hand in the lake water. "This lake is freshwater! A large city would have this as its drinking water." (Over the past two millennia, Lake Mariout has become saline, but it was fresh in Alexander's day.)

"And, of course, the Nile is the conduit to Memphis and the rest of Egypt. I can't imagine why the Egyptians never built a major city here," Ptolemy mused.

"Well, I'm going to! I'll call it Alexandria. It will be the jewel of Egypt! I have great plans for Alexandria. It'll be the busiest and most prosperous port on the Mediterranean."

Alexander pointed to a small island less than a mile from the isthmus. "Wouldn't that be a fantastic location for a lighthouse? We could build a causeway from here to there."

Alexander jumped out of the boat to the shore and scouted the area. He excitedly walked in a large circle, pointing out the boundaries of his city. His men hurried behind him with stakes, marking the places he named.

"I'll build the agora here! People will assemble to hear speeches, worship the gods, and watch entertainment and athletic contests. We'll have stalls for the merchants and nearby workshops."

Ptolemy scribbled notes as the enthusiastic Alexander dashed around. "Here! We'll erect temples in this area. We'll build a temple to the Egyptian goddess Isis on that little island. We need to show our appreciation of the Egyptian culture. But, of course, we'll have our Greek gods."

Alexander rattled off a list of how many temples to build and which Greek god each temple would honor.

"And, of course, we'll need a wall. Not just one—we'll have two walls! We'll build one inside the other for better protection. First thing, though, we'd better consult the priests! I want to ensure the gods like these plans."

The diviners offered sacrifices on the site and examined the entrails of the sacrificial animals. "All is well," the priests nodded. "The omens are favorable. The gods will be happy with temples and a new city here."

One of the soothsayers, Aristander the Telmissian, assured Alexander, "This city will be prosperous in every way, but especially regarding the fruit of the earth. It will grow enough grain to feed Egypt and other lands."

Alexander clapped his hands in glee and dashed back to make more plans for his city. His men had run out of stakes, so they resorted to throwing barley on the ground to mark out the outer and inner walls.[1]

---

[1] Arrian, "Alexander the Great," chapters I and II.

Alexander organized workers to lay the foundations of the city. Yet, after a couple of days, ever restless, Alexander was ready to press on. "I want to go to Libya! I hear that the temple of Amun in the Siwa Oasis gives exact information when you ask it a question. Did you know the hero Perseus consulted it?"

Ptolemy nodded. "And Heracles."

"Well, then, it's settled! Both are my ancestors, you know."

They sailed along the coast to Libya, then marched inland, getting lost in the desert. Ptolemy reported that two serpents hissed at them and led the way. Alexander was only in North Africa for a few months. Soon, he would lead his expedition to central Asia. Before leaving Egypt, he appointed Cleomenes as nomarch (governor) of northern Egypt and put him in charge of building Alexandria. Cleomenes was Greek and had grown up in the Greek colony of Naucratis, Egypt, up the Nile from Alexandria. Alexander appointed Dinocrates of Rhodes as the architect for the new city.

An artist's interpretation of how Alexandria may have looked[10]

Alexandria's Early Days

Dinocrates laid out the new city with a "Hippodamian" grid plan in a rectangular shape. It had straight streets intersecting others at right angles and an open agora area in the center. The Canopic Way, Alexandria's man thoroughfare, ran east and west through the city's center. Crates of Olynthus, a hydraulic engineer, designed Alexandria's sewers. An efficient drainage system was especially critical as Alexandria sat on swampy land. Dinocrates also built a three-quarter mile causeway called the Heptastadion from the mainland to Pharos Island, the city's port.

Cleomenes decided that the new city needed people to live in it, so he wanted to move the population of Canopus, an ancient Egyptian town about sixteen miles east, to Alexandria. Homer said King Menelaus built Canopus during the Trojan War, and it served as the major trade center on Egypt's coast. However, it had suffered earthquakes and tsunamis, perhaps one reason the Egyptians hadn't built a major city in the region.

Rising sea levels threatened to submerge Canopus, yet its citizens were indignant when ordered to leave their ancient home. They bribed Cleomenes to let them stay in their hometown, and he initially agreed. Cleomenes was known for extorting people to build his personal wealth. For instance, a crocodile ate one of his sons, so he commanded the Egyptians to kill all the crocodiles. Yet, the Egyptian priests considered crocodiles sacred and refused. Instead, they gave Cleomenes a big payoff to save the crocodiles, which Cleomenes accepted.

As Alexandria's construction continued, Cleomenes again demanded that the citizens of Canopus move to the new city or pay another hefty sum. They could not produce the money this time, so most of the population moved to Alexandria.

Meanwhile, Alexander was on his expedition to the Indian subcontinent. When he returned to Babylon in 323 BCE, he chastised Cleomenes for accepting bribes. Alexander's closest friend, Hephaestion, had suddenly died a few months earlier, and Alexander had asked the oracle at Siwa to grant divine status to his dear friend. He wrote Cleomenes with a command to build a magnificent monument to Hephaestion:

"Use Dinocrates as its architect. I'll overlook your unacceptable behavior if you zealously perform this to my satisfaction."

Alexander never saw his new city, the Jewel of the Mediterranean, as his untimely death cut off his plans to return to Egypt.

How did Alexandria become Egypt's capital?

After hashing out the details of the Partition of Babylon, Ptolemy traveled to Egypt to claim his piece of the empire. Memphis had been Egypt's capital, on and off, over three millennia. It had a distinguished history. Yet, Memphis also had priests so powerful they had essentially run the country, or parts of it, for centuries.

Ptolemy felt that the best course of action was a fresh start. He planned to forge a new kingdom that blended the best of Egyptian culture with Hellenism, the Greek culture. Ptolemy had shared Alexander's enthusiasm for building Alexandria on the Mediterranean coast. The westernmost Canopic branch of the Nile (almost entirely silted up today) was the water highway to the rest of Egypt. The Mediterranean linked Egypt to Greece, Phoenicia, Syria, Carthage, Sicily, and beyond. The trade would make Alexandria unimaginably rich. Yes! He would move Egypt's capital to Alexandria—a new city for a new era!

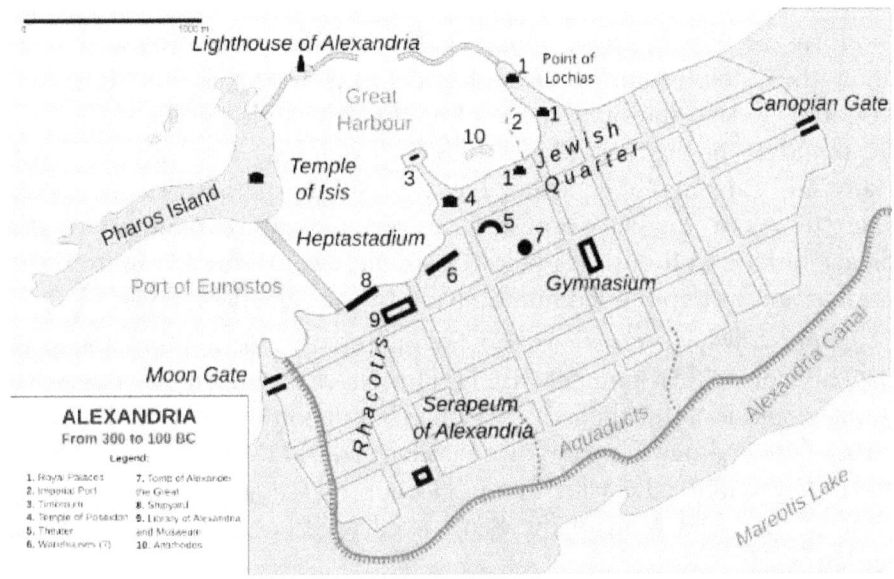

Alexandria's layout[11]

What made Alexandria exceptional?

Ptolemy also envisioned Alexandria as a vibrant center of scholarly studies and artistic exchange. He immediately set about attracting scholars and artists from around the Mediterranean. He brought in scientists, mathematicians, philosophers, architects, and other brilliant thinkers, cementing Alexandria's status as one of the ancient world's most illustrious cities. Alexandria soon reigned as the ancient world's new artistic and scientific powerhouse. The stunning metropolis grew to a population of half a million with thriving commerce.

The Gate of the Sun welcomed visitors into its eastern walls. The Jewish Quarter was near the sea in the northeastern part of the city. To its west was the Macedonian Barracks, a "museum" (temple to the Muses), and the ancient world's most extensive library. The Lochias Peninsula jutted into the sea with the palace and an elaborate dining hall. The Sema, Alexander's tomb, was either on the peninsula or in the city's center. His tomb was intact until at least 360 CE. Eventually, it was lost to earthquakes, tsunamis, and warfare. The city also had an art gallery, botanical gardens, an observatory, and a zoo.

Why was the Lighthouse of Alexandria such a famous landmark?

Diodorus Siculus, a first-century BCE historian, wrote that a voyage along the Mediterranean coast from Libya to Syria was long and arduous. He said the only safe landing was Alexandria's Pharos harbor. He pointed out that a hidden sandbank extended along Egypt's coast. Many ship captains thought they had escaped the perilous storms at sea when they saw Egypt's shores. However, they were unaware of the danger lurking in the waters below. Countless ships ran aground on the sandbar and were pounded into oblivion by the relentless waves.[i]

Egypt's low-lying coastline had few landmarks for a ship captain to plan his course. Around 900 BCE, Homer wrote in the *Odyssey* that sailors would look for the island of Pharos and come ashore in the "snug harbor." They knew the lake on the other side of the isthmus had fresh water they could take with them. Homer said that the shape-shifting Proteus, the "Old Man of the Sea," lived on Pharos island, where he herded seals.[ii]

Alexander had envisioned a lighthouse on Pharos, and Ptolemy set out to fulfill his dream. Pharos was already a well-known harbor, and he would capitalize on that. Ptolemy started the project using Sostratus of Cnidus as its architect. Ptolemy I died before its completion, but his son, Ptolemy II, finished the lighthouse, which rose 330 feet into the sky. The workers used marble blocks cemented together with lead mortar.

---

[i] Diodorus, *Library of History*, Volume I.
[ii] Homer, *The Odyssey*, trans. Samuel Butler. Internet Classics Archive, Book IV, 55. http://classics.mit.edu/Homer/odyssey.html.

An artistic representation of the Lighthouse of Alexandria[12]

The Lighthouse of Alexandria had three stories. The square-shaped lower level was the widest and tallest. The middle story was octagonal and slightly narrower than the bottom level. The top layer was round and had an enormous, curved mirror that reflected the sun by day and a lit fire at night. Sailors could see the lighthouse from thirty-five miles away. At its top was a statue of the Greek god Zeus. The Greek historian Herodotus listed it as one of the Seven Wonders of the World.

The remarkable Lighthouse of Alexandria guided the way to the Pharos harbor through the three centuries of the Ptolemy Kingdom and beyond. It captured Julius Caesar's admiration. He had a small-scale model with a burning light inside built for his triumphal parade through Rome. The top of the lighthouse was reportedly damaged in the Byzantine Era (beginning 395 CE) by treasure hunters who believed jewels were hidden inside. A series of earthquakes caused it to crumble partially, although its lower level still stood in 1182 CE. The Muslims installed a small mosque at its top. In 1375 CE, a devastating earthquake reduced the lighthouse to rubble. Sultan Qaitbay used its stones in the following century to build a fort.

Alexandria, the Jewel of the Mediterranean, survived and thrived to the present day. It reigns as the largest city on the Mediterranean, covering twenty-five miles of Egypt's coastline. In 2015, Egypt's Supreme Council of Antiquities approved a plan to rebuild the Lighthouse of Alexandria.

Chapter 3: The First Five Ptolemaic Rulers

The Ptolemaic Kingdom's first century was its glory days. The government was efficient, and the economy was healthy. It was a time of stunning scholarly breakthroughs. Greeks relocated to Egypt in droves, doubling its population and dramatically changing its demographics. Yet, eventually, the golden era began unraveling. Debauched kings, inept regents, and messy family feuds all took a toll. Meanwhile, Rome was morphing from a modest city-state into an empire. Egypt didn't notice until it was too late.

Ptolemy I Soter's Consolidated Kingdom (306-283 BCE)

One of Ptolemy's first acts as Egypt's governor was to execute Cleomenes. He detested Cleomenes's blatant bribery and believed he was a spy for Perdiccas. The Egyptians, who had suffered under Cleomenes, breathed a sigh of relief.

Once word got out that Alexander IV was dead, Antigonus crowned himself king over his vast swathe of Asia in 306 BCE. Ptolemy's officers leaped into action: "If Antigonus can be king, so can Ptolemy!" The other Diadochi quickly followed suit. In 304 BCE, the Egyptians crowned Ptolemy I as their pharaoh. He took the Egyptian throne name Meriamun Setepenra ("beloved of Amun, Chosen by Ra") and minted the first coins with his image.

As the "game of thrones" raged between the Diadochi, Ptolemy occasionally inserted himself. In 304 BCE, Ptolemy rescued the island of Rhodes from an attack by Antigonus and Demetrius. The grateful citizens of Rhodes gave Ptolemy the divine title of "Soter," or "Savior." In 302 BCE, Ptolemy invaded Phoenicia and southern Syria. By 295, Ptolemy controlled Tyre, Sidon, and the island of Cyprus.

Ptolemy I's coin[18]

In 320 BCE, Ptolemy I arrived in Jerusalem on the Jewish Sabbath, pretending he was coming to offer sacrifices. The Jews fell for it. It never occurred to them that Ptolemy intended to take Jerusalem. It was their day of rest, and they offered little resistance. Ptolemy rounded up captives from Judea and Samaria for his military. He gave them citizenship in Egypt if they swore fidelity to him.[i]

Ptolemy wrote a history of how Alexander conquered the Persian Empire. He included the part he played as an officer and eyewitness. This book has been lost. However, it was the primary source for Arrian's second-century CE history of Alexander. Ptolemy respected the Egyptian religion and restored temples the Persians had torn down. He wanted the Egyptians to accept him as their legitimate pharaoh.

The Last of the Diadochi

Ptolemy's oldest son from Eurydice, his third wife, was Ptolemy Ceraunus (Thunderbolt). He and his brother Meleager were meant to be the heir and the spare. However, Ptolemy then married his fourth wife, Berenice. He elevated Philadelphus, his son with Berenice, over his older sons. A power struggle ensued between the sons of both marriages.

---

[i] Flavius Josephus, *The Antiquities of the Jews,* trans. William Whiston (Project Gutenberg eBook, 2001), Book XII: chapter 1.

Meleager paced back and forth. "We've got to get out of Egypt! Berenice won't stop at anything. Especially you, Ceraunus! You were supposed to be crown prince. You're in mortal danger."

Ceraunus and Meleager fled Egypt, but Philadelphus killed their two younger brothers. Ceraunus escaped to Macedonia, ruled by his father's old friend, Lysimachus. Ceraunus's sister, Lysandra, was the wife of Lysimachus's oldest son, Agathocles. Lysimachus welcomed him warmly. However, Ceraunus soon realized his new situation was just as awkward and dangerous as the one he'd escaped. When Lysandra and Ceraunus were alone, she explained the palace intrigue to her brother.

"It's complicated and dangerous, Ceraunus. King Lysimachus has arranged a marriage between Agathocles's sister, Arsinoe I, and our half-brother, Philadelphus. It gets worse! Lysimachus just married a new wife, and you'll never guess who she is: Arsinoe II!"

"Arsinoe II! Our half-sister and Berenice's daughter?"

"Yes, Ceraunus! She's just as bad as Berenice! She's launched a campaign against my husband, Agathocles. You wouldn't believe the horrible things she's saying about him. Ceraunus, I'm terrified of what will happen!"

Within a few days, Lysandra's worst fears came true. Lysimachus executed Agathocles. He believed his wife over his son. Ceraunus fled with Lysandra to Babylon and the court of Seleucus, another of Ptolemy I's fellow officers under Alexander. Seleucus now ruled western and central Asia.

Seleucus I[14]

Their arrival played right into Seleucus's hands. He was looking for an excuse to attack Lysimachus. He also toyed with thoughts of invading Egypt, as Ptolemy I had recently died. In 281 CE, Seleucus and Ceraunus shattered Lysimachus's army in the Battle of Corupedium in Anatolia. It was the last battle of the Diadochi. A javelin impaled Lysimachus, killing him. Lysimachus was eighty years old, and Seleucus was seventy-seven.

Seleucus crossed the Hellespont into Europe and took Thrace. His next target was Macedonia, but Ptolemy Ceraunus cut his plans short. As Seleucus was offering sacrifices, Ceraunus stabbed him in the back. Ptolemy Ceraunus then crowned himself king of Macedonia and renounced all claims to the Egyptian throne.

Lysimachus's death left Ceraunus's half-sister Arsinoe II a widow. Despite their hostile history, Ceraunus shockingly proposed to Arsinoe, and she accepted. Why? They both had a tenuous hereditary claim to Macedonia's throne. If they married, it would double the strength of their claim. However, the marriage almost immediately imploded when Ceraunus discovered Arsinoe II and her sons were plotting against him. One account says it was on their wedding day. Ceraunus killed two of Arsinoe's sons, and Arsinoe fled to Egypt and married her full brother, Ptolemy II, who was now Egypt's pharaoh.

Ceraunus's reign as Macedonia's king didn't last long. The Galatians invaded in 279 BCE, and Ceraunus lost his head in the bloodbath.

Ptolemy II Philadelphus (284-246 BCE)

Ptolemy II Philadelphus[15]

While all the drama played out with Ceraunus in Europe and Asia, his younger half-brother, Philadelphus, began his reign in Egypt. Philadelphus was born in 309 BCE on the island of Kos in the Aegean Sea. Why was he born there and not in Egypt? The other Diadochi were fighting in Babylon, and Ptolemy invaded the Aegean when they were not paying attention. Berenice accompanied him, which seems bizarre given her pregnancy. Perhaps she was nervous about staying in Egypt with her rival, Eurydice.

Three brilliant Greek tutors schooled Philadelphus. Philitas of Cos was a renowned poet who spearheaded the development of the Library of Alexandria. Zenodotus of Ephesus was a student of Philitas and one of the library's first librarians. Strato of Lampsacus was a scholar with a keen interest in natural science. Through their influence, Philadelphus developed a deep appreciation of the arts and sciences. He led Egypt into the golden age of the Ptolemaic Kingdom.

Ptolemy I crowned Ptolemy II Philadelphus as king in 284 BCE when he was twenty-five. Philadelphus co-reigned with his father until Ptolemy I's death two years later. In the same year, Philadelphus's first wife, Arsinoe I (Lysimachus's daughter), gave birth to his oldest son, Ptolemy III Euergetes.

Palace politics took a menacing twist five years later. Ptolemy II's older sister, Arsinoe II, returned to Egypt after Lysimachus's death and her brief marriage to Ceraunus. She brought her son by Lysimachus, Ptolemy Epigonos.

Arsinoe I knew the insidious threat Arsinoe II's arrival presented. However, she was helpless to escape her rival's evil schemes. Arsinoe II convinced Ptolemy II that Arsinoe I was plotting against him. Ptolemy II exiled his first wife to Coptos, Egypt, five hundred miles up the Nile. He then married Arsinoe II, his full sister, and made her his co-regent. The name "Philadelphus" means "sibling-lover" in Koine Greek. The Greeks thought Ptolemy's marriage to his sister was scandalous, but the Egyptians just shrugged. Their pharaohs had been marrying their sisters since the Old Kingdom.

Ptolemy II Philadelphus and Arsinoe II had no children together. They may not have consummated their incestuous marriage. Arsinoe II was already in her forties and may have been past child-bearing age. Ptolemy II adopted Ptolemy Epigonos, her son by Lysimachus. "He will be Egypt's next king!" he promised his sister-wife. He had made Ptolemy Epigonos his co-regent.

However, the relationship fell apart when Ptolemy II sent Epigonos to Miletus in western Anatolia to spy out the political situation there. Epigonos joined forces with the tyrant Timarchus against Ptolemy. Timarchus died in the ensuing war, and Ptolemy II cut Epigonos off as his co-regent. However, he graciously gave Epigonos the city of Telmessos on Anatolia's Mediterranean coast, which had once belonged to Epigonos's birth father, Lysimachus. Epigonos ruled it as a client king under Ptolemy II.

Euergetes, Ptolemy II's oldest son by Arsinoe I, was his heir again. After forty years of ruling Egypt, Ptolemy II died in 246 BCE. He was buried in the Sema, the mausoleum where Ptolemy I had buried Alexander the Great.

A double cameo with Ptolemy II & Arsinoe II[16]

Besides his wives, Ptolemy II also had at least eleven concubines or lesser wives. His Macedonian concubine, Bilistiche, entered the Olympic chariot races and won several events. Ptolemy II created an Egyptian version of the Olympic Games called the Ptolemaieia, which met every four years in Alexandria. Its opening ceremonies included a lavish parade with over one hundred chariots pulled by elephants, antelope, ostriches, gnus, and zebras. Dancers, acrobats, and athletes entertained the crowds. Servants displayed Egypt's war treasures, and Ptolemy II's soldiers marched in full regalia.

Ptolemy II encouraged immigrants to Egypt from Greece, Macedonia, and West Asia. He especially wanted seasoned soldiers, although he also used Egyptian troops. He freed the Jews whom his father brought to Egypt as military conscripts. Some returned to Judea, but others preferred the exciting trade and scholarly hub of Alexandria. He had whole units of Jewish soldiers in his army, now volunteers.

Under Ptolemy II, Alexandria's library became a hotspot for scientists and mathematicians. They discussed and developed new theories, making astounding breakthroughs. Ptolemy II brought famous Greek poets like Apollonius of Rhodes, Callimachus, and Theocritus to Alexandria.

Ptolemy III Euergetes[17]

Ptolemy III Euergetes and His Remarkable Queen, Berenice II (246-222 BCE)

The name "Euergetes" meant "benefactor" or "one who does good deeds." Ptolemy III earned this name by lifting the Ptolemaic Dynasty to incredible heights in territory and economics. His childhood had been chaotic due to his stepmother forcing his mother into exile. He probably thought he had lost any chance of becoming Egypt's next king. And then it happened! His stepbrother, Epigonos, made the disastrous decision to oppose his father. Suddenly, Euergetes was elevated to crown prince and became engaged to Berenice II.

Berenice was probably the best thing that ever happened to Ptolemy III Euergetes. She was queen of Cyrene, an ancient Greek colony on Libya's Mediterranean Coast. Ptolemy I had captured it and written a new constitution for the city. When Cyrene rebelled, Ptolemy I sent Magus, his stepson by Berenice I of Egypt, to quell the rebels. Magus became Cyrene's governor, and after Ptolemy I died, crowned himself king of Cyrene. He even tried to invade Egypt, which did not go well for him. Yet, Ptolemy II was Magus's half-brother. The two kings reconciled, and Magus held Cyrene.

Berenice II was the only child of Magus and his queen, Apama II. Ptolemy II and Magus arranged for Ptolemy III to marry Berenice. However, after Magus died, his widow, Apama II, broke off Berenice's engagement to Euergetes. Instead, she arranged a marriage with Demetrius the Fair, grandson of Antigonus the One-eyed. Cyrene's citizens disliked her new husband. "He thinks more of himself than he ought. Furthermore, he's too heavy-handed! She should have married Ptolemy III," people whispered. "Demetrius is insufferable!"

Berenice had a hunch that something worse was happening. Her suspicions turned out to be true when she caught her handsome husband cheating on her—with her own mother! She called her guards to her mother's room. As the men burst into the room, Berenice cried, "Spare my mother!"

Apama tried to cover Demetrius with her own body. Nevertheless, it was hopeless. The guards ran Demetrius through as Apama screamed.[i]

"Now I will marry the man my father wanted me to marry," Berenice declared. She sailed to Alexandria, where a delighted Ptolemy III received her.

---

[i] Justinus, *Epitome of Pompeius Trogus' Philippic Histories*, trans. J. S. Watson (1853), 26.3. https://www.attalus.org/translate/justin4.html#26.1.

Ra, the Egyptian god of the sun and kingship, with Ptolemy III and Berenice II[18]

"She murdered her first husband! Is our king safe?" people whispered anxiously. With few friends in Egypt, Berenice had to forge a path for herself, which she did with aplomb. She surrounded herself with poets and scholars at the Library of Alexandria, who enshrined her charm, grace, modesty, and strength of character in dozens of poems. They championed Berenice as a loving wife and excellent mother to her six children—the ideal Greek woman. However, Berenice was also sophisticated and complex, a woman who navigated through treachery, court intrigues, and betrayal by those closest to her.

Yes, it was a political marriage, but it also was a love match—at least, it quickly grew into one. Ptolemy III never married anyone else, although both Egyptian and Macedonian traditions permitted multiple wives. No one ever mentioned him having mistresses or concubines. They had a large family together, and Berenice actively participated in government.

A few months after he married Berenice, Ptolemy III got embroiled in the Third Syrian War. His sister, Berenice Syra, was the wife of Antiochus II Theos, king of the Seleucid Empire in West Asia. After Berenice Syra became pregnant, Antiochus left her for his first wife,

Laodice. "You must return to Berenice!" Ptolemy III scolded. "We had a deal!" Antiochus refused and, shortly after, suddenly died.

"He must have been poisoned!" people whispered. "He was barely forty years old!"

"But who would kill him?"

"I'm guessing it was Laodice. I heard he was planning to go back to Berenice, and Laodice was jealous."

"But I thought he only married Berenice for her money. You know, she brought that huge dowry with her."

"Maybe, but Berenice's brother, Ptolemy III, insisted they reconcile, or Antiochus would have had to return the dowry. Laodice feared he would make Berenice's son the next king instead of her son, Callinicus."

Berenice Syra desperately sent messages to her brother Ptolemy to rescue her. "Laodice will murder me and my little son. Come quickly!"

Ptolemy III mustered his army to march north to his sister and nephew in Antioch, Syria. Queen Berenice cut off her hair as a sacrifice for her husband's safe return. She placed her hair in Aphrodite's temple in Alexandria as a votive offering. However, when the priests entered the temple the following morning, the hair had disappeared!

Drachma coin with Berenice II of Egypt[19]

The priests and court were mystified. What happened to the hair? Finally, the court astronomer, Conon of Samos, produced the answer as night fell. "Look! Up in the northern sky, between Leo and Boötes. What do you see? It's a new constellation! Aphrodite placed it there. That's Berenice's hair! The goddess has shown her favor to Berenice for her sacrifice. Her prayers will come true! Her husband and our king will return safely." The poets Callimachus and Catullus both wrote about "Berenice's lock."

Meanwhile, Ptolemy III was leading his army up the Mediterranean coast. When he reached Antioch, he received devastating news. Laodice's henchmen had already killed his sister and her little son, Antiochus. Laodice and her sons were in the north, hiding out in Anatolia. The good news was that the Syrian forces loyal to Berenice had taken Celicia. It served as a buffer zone between Syria and Laodice's army.

Ptolemy III was too late to rescue his sister, but conditions were ripe for taking the rest of the Seleucid Empire. He set out on the most jaw-dropping conquest of any Ptolemaic ruler. With his infantry, cavalry, and war elephants, he captured Syria and Mesopotamia. Crowned "King of Asia," he even claimed to have conquered Persia and Bactria (Afghanistan, Tajikistan, and Uzbekistan). Ptolemy III hunted down the sacred treasures the Persians stole from the Egyptian temples centuries earlier and shipped them home.

Just then, however, he received word of an uprising back home. The native Egyptians had grown weary of the Ptolemaic Kingdom's heavy taxes, which had grown heavier when Ptolemy III needed to fund his new war. Moreover, the annual Nile flooding had failed in 245 BCE. The lakes further south that fed the Nile tributaries had not received enough rain. The Egyptians manipulated the annual Nile flooding to saturate their fields before planting. If the Nile did not flood, they could not grow the crops they depended on for food and trade with other countries.

What disrupted the rainfall south of Egypt? Ice cores from Greenland and Antarctica show that major volcanic eruptions occurred in 247 BCE, triggering cooler air from the ash and sulfur dioxide circulating the earth and filtering sunlight. This cooler air disrupted the African monsoon. Thus, faraway volcanoes triggered a famine in Egypt that forced Ptolemy III to abandon the war and return home—just as he was on the brink of capturing the entire Seleucid Empire.[i]

The Syrian War ended in 241 BCE when the Ptolemaic Kingdom and the Seleucids agreed to a peace treaty. Ptolemy III kept the land he conquered in Anatolia and Syria. Now, he controlled the Mediterranean coastline from Libya to Anatolia. He also kept Antioch, Alexandria's biggest competitor in trade and scholarly pursuits.

Ptolemy III continued to build up Alexandria's reputation as the Mediterranean's cultural star. He encouraged the works of mathematicians, geographers, and astronomers in his court, like Apollonius of Perga, Conon of Samos, and Eratosthenes.

His father's goal was to include a copy of every book in the world in the Library of Alexandria. Apparently, that library was getting too full, so Ptolemy III built a second one in the Temple of Serapis. He copied every scroll that entered Alexandria's port. He kept the original for his library and gave the copy to the owner. Ptolemy III often had to pay a massive fine for keeping the precious originals. These included the official manuscripts of the Greek tragedy writers Sophocles, Aeschylus, and Euripides.

Ptolemy III died in 221 BCE, and his oldest son, Philopator, became the next king.

Silver coin of Ptolemy IV Philopator[20]

---

[i] Manning, J. G., et al. "Volcanic Suppression of Nile Summer Flooding Triggers Revolt and Constrains Interstate Conflict in Ancient Egypt," *Nature Communications* 8, no. 900 (2017), https://doi.org/10.1038/s41467-017-00957-y.

Ptolemy IV Philopator Purges the Royal Family (221-204 BCE)

Philopator, whose name means "father-loving," became the fourth king of the Ptolemaic Kingdom in his early twenties. He married his full sister, Arsinoe III, and they had one son in 210 BCE: Ptolemy V. Philopator's mistress was Agathoclea. Her brother Agathocles and another friend, Sosibius, were his closest advisors and led him down a dark path. Philopator let these two men run the kingdom while he abandoned himself to a life of ease, indulging his every desire. Sosibius's name appeared on royal documents more than Philopator's.

Philopater might have loved his father, but not the rest of his family. His advisors got annoyed when the king's mother, Berenice II, and other family members questioned what Agathocles and Sosibius were doing. With the king's permission, they poisoned Berenice II. They poured boiling water over Philopater's younger brother, Magus, the army commander. They also killed Lysimachus, Philopater's great-uncle.

The killing spree was not over. Sosibius thought Cleomenes, a king of the Greek city-state of Sparta, presented a threat. He had achieved remarkable reforms and begun conquering the rest of Greece until he lost to the Macedonians and Achaeans. He had fled to Egypt, where Ptolemy III gave him refuge. Ptolemy III died soon after.

Egged on by his advisors, Ptolemy IV put Cleomenes under house arrest. Why? Alexandria's army had many mercenary soldiers from the Sparta area. Ptolemy IV feared the soldiers would be more loyal to Cleomenes than him if Cleomenes sparked a revolt.

Cleomenes did attempt a revolt when Ptolemy IV and his minions were out of town. Cleomenes and the thirteen Spartans with him broke free. With daggers held high, they raced through Alexandria's streets, calling, "Rise up! Be like true Greeks! Champion liberty! Together, we can set up a free state. We'll overturn the Ptolemaic despots!"

The Alexandrians looked curiously at the Spartans. Yes, the Alexandrians were Greeks, but they had been a kingdom for a century. Greek-style democracy was a foreign concept, and revolution wasn't their thing. "These Spartans are rather eccentric, don't you think?" the Alexandrians murmured.

When they saw it was hopeless, Cleomenes and his men fell on their daggers.

Ptolemy IV won an unexpected victory against Antigonus III of the Seleucid Empire. However, rather than pressing his advantage and crippling the Seleucids, he made peace. Ptolemy IV continued to lead successful expeditions in Greece. However, he was disinterested in ruling the Greek states. He merely demanded terms of peace. During this time, the Roman Republic had strengthened and was at war with Carthage on North Africa's coast, west of Egypt. Ptolemy IV kept his options open by remaining neutral yet friendly with both sides.

A drawing of Ptolemy IV's Thalamegos, his luxury, two-hulled catamaran[21]

Around 206 BCE, internal revolts rocked Egypt, just as they had in the reign of Ptolemy III. This time, the Egyptians of southern Egypt declared independence. Their leader, Horwennefer, crowned himself Egypt's new pharaoh in Thebes. Native Egyptians now ruled southern Egypt, and the Greeks ruled northern Egypt.

While all this was going on, Ptolemy IV and his wife died in mysterious circumstances. Some thought Ptolemy IV may have died from something related to his obesity or heavy drinking. Yet, he and his wife died around the same time. Were they poisoned? Some whispered about a fire in the palace. No one knew, especially since Sosibius kept their deaths a secret for weeks.

Ptolemy V Epiphanes and His Bungling Regents (203-180 BCE)

The two villains, Agathocles and Sosibius, stood in the palace court with five-year-old Epiphanes between them, wearing a miniature royal diadem on his tiny head. Two silver urns rested on a table next to them. The nobility of Alexandria stood waiting. Sosibius cleared his throat and spoke.

> "We regret to inform you that our Father-loving gods, King Ptolemy IV and Queen Arsinoe III, have left us for heaven. Their ashes are here, and we will give them a royal burial in the Sema, next to Alexander the Great. Ptolemy V Epiphanes is our new king. Here is Ptolemy IV's will. He has appointed Agathocles and me as guardians of his son. Furthermore, Agathocles will be regent until King Ptolemy V comes of age."[i]

Everyone looked at each other, shaking their heads and whispering. "It's all so sudden! They haven't even explained what happened to our king and queen. And we already hate Agathocles! He's too prideful. It was bad enough when Epiphanes was alive. Now, Agathocles will have free rein for his villainy!"

Agathocles and Sosibius set to work exiling any possible contenders from Egypt. They were nervous that the power vacuum might incite an invasion from Rome, Macedonia, or the Seleucids. Yet, the people had endured enough. The citizens of Alexandria revolted. Led by the army commander Tlepolemus, they dragged Agathocles out of the palace and tore him to pieces. Sosibius had recently died, and his son sided with the revolutionaries. They made Tlepolemus regent for little Ptolemy V, now seven years old.

Gold coin of Ptolemy V, the child king[ii]

---

[i] E. R. Bevan, *The House of Ptolemy* (Methuen Publishing, 1927), chap. VIII, https://penelope.uchicago.edu/Thayer/E/Gazetteer/Places/Africa/Egypt/_Texts/BEVHOP/6*.html.

Tlepolemus botched his role as regent. He ignored state affairs and spent too much time partying and playing ball. His neglect destabilized Egypt, so in 201 BCE, Aristomenes of Alyzia took over as regent.

Antiochus III (the Great) of the Seleucid Empire and Philip V of Macedonia jumped at the chance to take advantage of the upheaval. They met in 200 BCE to plot out their strategy.

"Philip, we both know Egypt is weak right now! Their king is only ten years old, and they keep changing regents. The entire Ptolemaic Empire outside of Egypt is ours for the taking."

"I agree, Antiochus! If we attack on different fronts simultaneously, we can divide it between ourselves."

Antiochus smiled. "I'll take Syria, Cyprus, Celicia, and Lycia."

Philip nodded. "And I'll take the rest of Anatolia, Thrace, and the Cyclades."

They launched the Second Macedonian War. Antiochus the Great easily took Syria. When he reached Judea in 198 BCE, the Jews threw open Jerusalem's gates, welcoming him as their conquering hero from the Egyptians. They never expected the horrors his son, Antiochus Epiphanes, would soon bring.

Meanwhile, Philip was making headway in the Aegean. But it didn't all go as planned. Rome got involved, having just wrapped up its war with Carthage. In two battles, the Romans killed most of Philips's men, forcing him to pull out of the war.

Ptolemy V turned fourteen in 196 BCE and was crowned Egypt's pharaoh at Memphis. The Egyptian priests gathered and passed

The Rosetta Stone of Ptolemy V Epiphanes[20]

the "Memphis Decree," carved on the Rosetta Stone. (This monument of polished black granodiorite is almost four feet high. It was once higher, but part of it broke off.) It had identical inscriptions written in three scripts: Egyptian hieroglyphics, Demotic (another Egyptian script), and Greek.

In all three scripts, the priests praised the king's kindness in releasing prisoners, outlawing forced labor, and restoring and rebuilding the Egyptian temples. They proclaimed Ptolemy V's new divine cult and ordered the temples throughout Egypt to install statues of their new king. (Two thousand years later, Napolean's army discovered the monument. The Rosetta Stone unlocked Egyptian hieroglyphics, enabling scholars to translate them.)

Antiochus made peace with Ptolemy V the following year, outraging the Romans. Antiochus kept Judea, Syria, and Anatolia, and Ptolemy got Antiochus's daughter, Cleopatra I ("the Syrian"), as his wife. She was only eight, so they waited two years to marry. The couple had two sons and a daughter, and all three ruled Egypt together.

Ptolemy V successfully took back southern Egypt by 186 BCE. He planned to take back Syria, Phoenicia, and Judea after Antiochus the Great died, but he himself died suddenly in 180 BCE at age thirty. Rumors were that his advisors poisoned him to avoid the heavy taxes needed for a new war. His death marked the beginning of the end for the Ptolemaic Kingdom. It stumbled along for another 150 years but never achieved its early kings' brilliance or massive territory.

Chapter 4: Cultural Fusion: Greek Influence on Egyptian Society

Ptolemy I's reign laid the groundwork for the unique Hellenistic-Egyptian civilization that would flourish under his successors. The Ptolemaic rulers blended Greek and Egyptian cultures to create a unique societal fabric. What did that look like? Was Greek or Egyptian the most common language? Who were the new gods? Did the Ptolemaic rulers follow Greek or Egyptian administrative styles? This chapter will spend some time answering these questions.

What was the relationship between Egypt and Greece before Ptolemy I?

From their early history, the Egyptians and Greeks had enjoyed a lively cultural interchange. The Minoans and Mycenaeans traded with Egypt in the Bronze Age (3300-1200 BCE). The Minoans of Crete (an island about halfway between Egypt and Greece) developed a hieroglyphic writing system that looked similar to Egyptian hieroglyphics. Yet, Cretan Hieroglyphic was phonetic and had only eighty-five symbols compared to over eight hundred symbols in Egyptian hieroglyphics.

Through this cultural interchange, some of the Greek and Egyptian mythology intermingled. For instance, the Egyptians had their own twist on Helen of Troy. In the Egyptian version, after kidnapping Helen from Sparta in Greece, Prince Paris meant to take her to Troy. However, a storm blew his ship to Egypt's coast. Helen privately told the Egyptian pharaoh, Seti II, that she had *not* gone with Paris willingly. She loved her husband, King Menelaus.

Seti took pity on Helen and hid her from Paris in a temple. His daughter, a high priestess, called up the god Thoth. He separated Helen's body from her "ka" or spirit. Her ka went with Paris to Troy, but Helen remained in Egypt for ten years while the Trojan War raged. Finally, at the war's end, a storm blew King Menelaus's ship to Egypt, where he reunited with Helen.[i]

About a thousand years before Ptolemy I became king, the Egyptian pharaoh Psamtik I permitted the Greeks of Miletus to establish a colony in Egypt. Their new city was Naucratis, on the westernmost Canopic branch of the Nile, about forty-five miles upstream from where Alexandria would one day be built. It grew into a lively trade center where Egyptian and Greek culture and knowledge interchanged.

Naucratis later became the home base for the Greek military unit. Greek mercenaries fought in the Egyptian forces for hundreds of years before Alexander arrived.

In 460 BCE, the Greeks sailed two hundred ships to Egypt to assist the Egyptian rebel leader, Inaros II, in evicting the hated Persians. The Athenian League had already driven the despised Persians from the Aegean Sea and felt invincible. Initially, they succeeded, killing a hundred thousand Persians and capturing or sinking eighty Persian ships. Yet, the Persians had an inexhaustible source of manpower. They sent three hundred more vessels and two hundred thousand men, viciously crushing the Egyptians and Greeks.

Who spoke which language?

Ptolemaic Egypt had two official languages: Egyptian and Koine Greek (the "common dialect"). Koine Greek had spread throughout the Middle East after Alexander the Great's conquests. For three centuries, it was the lingua franca of North Africa, West Asia, and Eastern Europe. A common language enabled the ancient Mediterranean world to surge ahead in trade and dramatically impacted the pursuit of knowledge.

Greek, the language of the royal court and the Greek administrators, was the primary language in Alexandria and Naucratis. The Ptolemaic

---

[i] Herodotus, *The Histories*, trans. George Rawlinson (Dutton & Co, 1862), 2:113-120, http://classics.mit.edu/Herodotus/history.html.

rulers imported Greek schoolteachers and gave them tax breaks.

Language divided the Egyptians and the Greeks of Egypt. About half of Egypt's population was still Egyptian. They primarily spoke Egyptian and wrote in the Egyptian Demotic script except for monuments, for which they used ancient hieroglyphics. Egyptian was the language of the temples and priesthood. Cleopatra VII, the last pharaoh, was the only ruler known to have learned the Egyptian language.

Speaking of Cleopatra, the name was Macedonian, not Egyptian. It meant "glory of the father." As you might have noticed, the Ptolemies liked to use the same names over and over. All the kings were named Ptolemy, a popular Macedonian name that meant "warrior." Alexander the Great's sister was Cleopatra, and the name was used repeatedly throughout the dynasty. Cleopatra VII was *the* Cleopatra, the one who married two of her brothers and carried on with Julius Caesar and Mark Antony. Her story is in chapter eight, which unwraps the decline and fall of the Ptolemaic Kingdom. Many other queens and princesses had the name Arsinoe or Berenice. Arsinoe was a Greek word that meant "enlightened woman," and Berenice meant "victory bringer."

As for legal affairs, the native Egyptians continued to follow their traditional laws. However, they also had to follow the royal laws of the Macedonian kings. If they had to write a contract, the language depended on whether it dealt with Egyptian or royal law. If the latter, they used Koine Greek.

Of course, plenty of people in Egypt were bilingual, simply for survival. Many Greeks married Egyptian women, so they had bilingual households. Most Egyptian administrators kept their jobs when Ptolemy I came into power, but now they had to communicate in two languages. Some folks even had two names—one Greek and one Egyptian.

How did cultural fusion impact architecture and art?

In the three centuries of Macedonian kings, art and architecture reflected both Greek and Egyptian styles. At first, the Ptolemaic kings continued the traditional Egyptian forms. The exception was Alexandria, with its mostly Greek population. This city mainly had Greek-style art and architecture. However, the Ptolemies built Egyptian-style statues of themselves in the harbor and several Egyptian-style temples.

Egyptian sistrum with Ptolemy I's cartouche on the handle[24]

Art and architecture were political in a sense. The Ptolemies wanted to present themselves as a continuation of the Egyptian pharaohs. For example, the Egyptians used a rattle called a sistrum when worshiping goddesses like Isis, Hathor, or Bastet. Ptolemy I had a sistrum made from faience or glazed pottery. His name was on the handle in Egyptian hieroglyphics inside a "cartouche," an oval that signified a pharaoh's name. The face on the rattle was the Egyptian goddess Hathor, and the style of the sistrum was traditional Egyptian. It symbolized Ptolemy I's continuation of Egyptian art and religion.

In the towns and cities where the Egyptians lived, the Ptolemies installed statues of themselves wearing the regalia of Egyptian pharaohs. They wanted to assure the Egyptians of their respect for their culture. Yet, by the second generation of Greek rule, statues had Egyptian poses and clothing but Greek hairstyles and facial features.

Ptolemy I and his successors rebuilt the Egyptian temples in the same style the Egyptians had used for centuries. Ptolemy VI Philometor built a new structure, the Temple of Kom Ombo, dedicated to the Egyptian falcon god Horus and the crocodile god Sobek.

This wall relief from the Kom Ombo temple shows Sobek (l) and the goddesses Isis and Hathor crowning a Ptolemaic pharaoh.[25]

How did the integration of Greek and Egyptian religions work?

The Egyptians continued to worship their gods, whom the Ptolemies respected. The Macedonian kings supported the temples and attended special ceremonies. The Greek population continued to worship their traditional gods. However, the Ptolemies also started new cults. Ptolemy I introduced the god Serapis to his Egyptian and Greek subjects. Serapis was a fusion of the supreme Greek god Zeus and the Egyptian gods Osiris and Apis. Osiris was the lord of the underworld and the firstborn of Egypt's gods. Apis was a bull and also a god of the underworld.

Serapis had a full beard and looked Greek. He balanced a large cup on his head, representing abundance and new life after death. He became a popular god in Greece and Rome.

According to Plutarch, Ptolemy I had dreamed of a colossal statue of Pluto (Hades), the Greek god of the underworld. Pluto told Ptolemy to bring his statue to Alexandria. Ptolemy was perplexed. He had no idea where the statue was! He started telling his friends about his dream. Finally, he told his friend Sosibius, who had traveled widely.

"Ptolemy! I saw an enormous statue in Sinope! Maybe it was the god in your dream."

"Really? Where is Sinope?" Ptolemy asked eagerly.

"It's on the Black Sea—a long way from here."

Despite the distance and danger of the sea journey, Ptolemy had his men sail to the Black Sea and steal the statue. When they returned to Egypt, Ptolemy called his Egyptian and Greek priests to inspect the statue. They agreed that it represented Osiris (or Pluto). So, Ptolemy built a gigantic temple for his stolen statue, which he named Serapis.[i]

Serapis [26]

The Egyptians considered their pharaohs to be earthly representations of the god Horus. They believed their pharaohs were part mortal and part god and were intermediaries between them and the gods. The Ptolemies latched on to this and encouraged the Egyptians to consider them divine. Ptolemy II elevated his sister and second wife, Arsinoe II, as the earthly representation of Isis and the Greek goddess Hera. He built a temple for her and held festivals in her honor. He issued coins with Arsinoe II wearing a goddess's diadem.

In 238 BCE, Ptolemy III's little girl, Berenice, died. A little later, Ptolemy III called an assembly of all Egypt's priests. The priests wrote the Decree of Canopus, which honored the dead little girl as a goddess. The decree also lauded Ptolemy III's military prowess. They described how he supported the Egyptian priesthood by returning the idols and other religious artifacts the Persians stole from Egypt. The priests

---

[i] Plutarch, "Moralia," *Isis and Osiris* (Loeb Classical Library, 1936), https://penelope.uchicago.edu/Thayer/e/roman/texts/plutarch/moralia/isis_and_osiris*/b.html.

thanked their pharaoh for importing grain to feed everyone when the Nile went nearly dry and famine struck. Most of the decree dealt with reforms among the priests, but it also added a leap day every four years to the 365-day year.

What was the bicultural administration like?

The Ptolemies went to great lengths to respect the ancient Egyptian culture, of which the Egyptians were inordinately proud. The Egyptians liked to point out that they had an advanced civilization way back when the "barbarian" Greeks had still not learned how to rid their beards of lice. The Ptolemies knew that trying to force Greek culture on the Egyptians was hopeless. Instead, they pretended to be Egyptians:[i]

> "Given that the maintenance of order depended on the existence of a legitimate pharaoh, the Egyptians were obliged to recognize the prevailing ruler as their Horus-King, for as long as he could not be replaced by another king. Conversely, foreign rulers also had to assume the religious role of the pharaoh, if they were to secure their success ... the Ptolemies took particular care to act as culturally relevant kings and, thus, gain acceptance (whenever possible) as the central figure of Egyptian religion."[ii]

When dealing with the Egyptians, the Ptolemies used the title pharaoh and dressed in Egyptian clothing.

In Alexandria, the Greeks called their rulers "basileus," which meant "monarch" in Greek. The Greeks had experimented with several styles of government since emerging from their Dark Ages. Athens had developed an early form of democracy. Sparta had two kings. Thebes had an oligarchy, or a council of aristocrats. Tyrants ruled Corinth for a few years. Macedonia had a traditional monarchy, the model the Ptolemies chose. A monarchy was also the system that Egypt had under their pharaohs until the Persians invaded.

Alexander the Great had rarely changed the existing systems in the conquered regions unless they weren't working. He usually kept what was already in place and tweaked it a bit. The Ptolemaic pharaohs did

---

[i] Philip Matyszak, *Greece Against Rome: The Fall of the Hellenistic Kingdoms 250-31 BC* (Pen & Sword Military, 2020).

[ii] Günther Hölbl, *A History of the Ptolemaic Empire*, trans. Tina Saavedra (Routledge, 2000), 1.

the same, mostly continuing the administrative system the Egyptians already had in place. For instance, their marriage and property laws stayed the same.

The Egyptians followed Egyptian law, while the Greek citizens followed Greek law and had their own courts. However, the Greeks were at the top of the administrative ladder and had special rights and privileges.

Most people in Egypt had always been farmers. The government, temples, and nobility owned nearly all the land, and the farmers worked as serfs. This system stayed the same in the Ptolemaic kingdom, except now the aristocrats and government were the Greeks.

How were Greek agricultural techniques blended with traditional Egyptian farming practices?

Ptolemy II and Ptolemy III rewarded their Macedonian military with land grants and established farm colonies for their Macedonian veterans. One large colony was Crocodilopolis (near today's Faiyum) in the lake region about eighty miles southwest of Memphis. It was named after the pet crocodile the local Egyptians worshiped and decorated with gold and gems. The Greeks also had garrisons around the country, with the surrounding land farmed by the Macedonian soldiers.

Egyptian farmer[87]

Egypt already had excellent farming techniques that took advantage of the annual Nile flooding. The Macedonians introduced some of their methods, and Egypt's agricultural production soared to new heights. For instance, in Crocodilopolis, the Greeks drained the swampland to use for fields. They built longer canal systems so farms could thrive further away from the Nile. The Ptolemies learned early on that the Nile sometimes didn't flood as it should, which devastated agricultural production and left the people starving. To offset this, the Ptolemaic rulers started stockpiling grain in the years of plenty to use during famines.

The Greeks brought new crops, like durum wheat, and increased sheep and goat herding for wool. The Egyptians liked drinking beer, but the Greeks preferred wine, so they introduced vineyards.

Chapter 5: The Great Library of Alexandria

As Alexander the Great shared his vision for Alexandria, he wanted it to rival Athens. "You must build a library and dedicate it to the Muses!" The first three Ptolemies made Alexander's dream a reality. They created the world's most extensive collection of scrolls, an incredible intellectual legacy. The Library of Alexandria transformed the city into the ancient world's creative hub. It drew scholars and poets from the Greek, Jewish, Roman, and Syrian cultures.

How was the library established?

As mentioned, the dream had started with Alexander, yet Ptolemy I and his immediate descendants put it into action. Ptolemy I built the "Museum" of Alexandria. In those days, a museum wasn't a collection of artifacts but a temple of the Muses—the nine Greek goddesses who inspired knowledge in the arts, literature, and science. The Alexandrian Museum was like a modern research university, where great minds came together to discuss the latest ideas and research.

Demetrius of Phalerum was a Greek philosopher and historian. For ten years, he was the governor of Athens under King Cassander of Macedon. Then, the political scene in Athens shifted. Forced into exile, Demetrius joined Ptolemy I in Egypt. The historian Strabo said that Demetrius created the museum, patterning it after Aristotle's school in Athens. The museum featured a covered walkway and a communal dining room. Most importantly, it had the library with thousands of carefully organized scrolls.

What the Great Library of Alexandria may have looked like[38]

No library in the ancient world came close to the Library of Alexandria's staggering collection. Its librarians zealously hunted down "every book in the world." One day, Ptolemy II met with his librarian, Demetrius of Phalerum.

"How many scrolls are in the library now?"

"Sire, we have more than two hundred thousand. I'm working day and night to reach my goal of a half million."

By Ptolemy III's reign, Callimachus, the librarian and poet, updated the count. "We now have four hundred thousand mixed scrolls and ninety thousand unmixed." A "mixed" scroll probably meant it contained a collection of works. An "unmixed" scroll was one book. They had almost achieved Demetrius's goal of a half-million scrolls.

Many classical works, including those of Homer, Plato, and Aristotle, were preserved, copied, and studied in Alexandria. These texts were later translated into Latin and Arabic, ensuring their survival through the Middle Ages.

How did its vast collection of scrolls contribute to various fields of study?

Scholars gathered to read the scrolls, translate works into Greek, and discuss them with other mental giants. The library's scholars surged ahead in the sciences, math, philosophy, and literature. It was a society of savants making unprecedented strides. With their brilliant minds, the library's resources, and a cross-disciplinary approach, they made one breathtaking breakthrough after another.

The scholars and intellectuals clustered in Alexandria's library fostered a vibrant academic community. As "Fellows of the Museum," they got free housing and didn't have to pay taxes. Chapter nine dives into the legacy of these scholars, including Euclid and Eratosthenes, who made strides in geometry. The mathematician and engineer, Hero of Alexandria, taught at the Museum in the Roman era. The Alexandrian Pleiad was a group of poets and writers of Greek tragedy that clustered at the library. Among

Demetrius of Phalerum[29]

them were Alexander Aetolus, Homerus the Younger, Lycophron, Philiscus of Corcyra, and Sositheus of Alexandria.

Who were some of the librarians?

The date for the library's founding is unclear, and sources disagree on who the first librarian was. Like Strabo, some say it was Demetrius of Phalerum, while others say it was Zenodotus of Ephesus. However, Zenodotus wasn't appointed the chief librarian until 284 BCE, a year before Ptolemy I died. Demetrius died in 280 BCE, so Demetrius and Zenodotus possibly served together for several years.

Zenodotus was an epic poet who edited Homer and organized and cataloged other poets. He divided Homer's poems into twenty-four books and gave lectures on Hesiod, Anacreon, and Pindar. His assistants were Alexander the Aetolian, who edited the Greek tragedies, and Lycophron, who worked with the comedies. Zenodotus assigned different literature genres to various rooms of the library and then organized them alphabetically. Each scroll had a small tag hanging from its end. It had the author's name and other information so the librarians could return it to the correct place. In addition to his librarian work, Zenodotus tutored Ptolemy II's children. Instructing the royal children became part of the job for future librarians.

Callimachus of Cyrene was a librarian during the reigns of Ptolemy II and III. However, no one mentioned he was the head librarian. Still, he did create a reference guide, something like a card catalog. Callimachus took Zenodotus's alphabetization to the next level by writing the *Pinakes*, a systematic list of the bibliographic information of every scroll in the library. The bibliographic information in the *Pinakes* filled 120 books. The shelves and bins holding the scrolls had tablets over them with their bibliographic information drawn from the *Pinakes*.

In addition to organizing the library, Callimachus was a prolific writer, producing over eight hundred poems, hymns, and works of prose. His favorite topic was the nature of beauty, as evidenced in his "Hymn to Apollo":

> "Begin, young men, begin the sacred song.
> Wake all your lyres, and to the dances throng,
> Rememb'ring still, the Pow'r is seen by none
> Except the just and innocent alone;
> Prepare your minds, and wash the spots away,
> That hinder men to view th' all-piercing ray,
> Lest ye provoke his fav'ring beams to bend
> On happier climes, and happier skies ascend"

Callimachus probably worked under Eratosthenes of Cyrene, who became the lead librarian toward the end of Ptolemy II's reign. Eratosthenes lived well into his eighties and continued as the librarian through the reigns of the subsequent three kings. He was a literary and scientific genius in multiple fields, including astronomy, math, geography, poetry, and music. He is best known for figuring out the earth's circumference. (Chapter nine digs into that.)

What scripture translation went into the library?

The library included scriptures from many religions translated into Greek. However, one was missing. In the "Letter of Aristeas," written around 180 BCE, one of Ptolemy II's courtiers told how he visited the library with the king one day.

Demetrius, the librarian, spoke up. "Sire, I'm told that the laws of the Jews deserve a place in your library."

Ptolemy II frowned. "What's prevented you from doing this?"

"They need to be translated," answered Demetrius. "You see, their scriptures are written in their ancient Hebrew language. It's similar to the early Syrian script, but hardly anyone uses it today."

Ptolemy II nodded and sent a letter to Eleazer, the high priest in Jerusalem:

> "Greetings and salutations. Many Jews live in our realm of Egypt, who the Persians carried off from Jerusalem. My father brought thousands more into Egypt as soldiers with a high wage. Others came as enslaved people. I have freed more than one hundred thousand captives and made reparation. Thousands of Jews are now in my army and official positions. I want your sacred law translated from Hebrew to Greek and added to my library. Please select six elders from each tribe who are skilled in your law and interpretation. I am sending a hundred talents of silver as an offering for your temple and its sacrifices."[i]

---

[i] *The Letter of Aristeas to Philocrates*, trans. R. H. Charles (1913), https://www.attalus.org/translate/aristeas1.html.

Some scholars question the authenticity of the Letter of Aristeas. However, Aristobulus of Alexandria included part of the letter in his writings about eighty years later Philo of Alexandria also mentioned the letter.

Ptolemy II housed the Jewish scholars on the island of Pharos. They translated the Torah (the first five books of the Old Testament) into Greek, and it went into the Library of Alexandria. Hebrew scholars translated the rest of the Jewish Tanakh (Old Testament) over the next few decades. The Greek translation is called the Septuagint (The Translation of the Seventy) in honor of the Jewish scholars sent to Egypt to begin its translation. Based on language analysis, the Greek translation of the Torah took place in the third century BCE.

The Greek translation of the Tanakh served as a valuable tool for Judaism in Egypt and elsewhere.

Tens of thousands of Jews lived in the northeastern Jewish quarter of Alexandria, which took up about a fifth of the city then. Even the Jews in Judea were rapidly becoming Hellenized under Ptolemaic rule. Their languages were Koine Greek and Aramaic (a relic of the Babylonian captivity).

Before long, synagogues in Egypt, Judea, and the rest of the eastern Mediterranean were using the Greek Septuagint version. Jesus read from the Greek Septuagint in the synagogue at Nazareth (Luke 4:16-21). The apostle Peter quoted from the Greek Septuagint (Acts 2:17-21), as did most New Testament writers.

Chapter 6: Ptolemaic Economy

Of all the Diadochi kingdoms, Egypt was the longest-lasting and, ultimately, the richest. Egypt's strategic position at the crossroads of major trade routes facilitated trade between Africa, Asia, and Europe. Egypt's grain was the gift of the Nile. The Ptolemies enhanced its production, so there was enough to feed Egypt plus export to Greece and Rome. The Ptolemaic Kingdom's stellar economic strategies grew and sustained its prosperity. The Ptolemaic kings used this wealth productively through financing infrastructure and promoting scholarly and cultural advances. They enhanced life for their people and built their influence in the ancient world.

Egypt Starts Using Money

Before the Greeks arrived, Egypt's use of coins was spotty. Most of the time, they just traded one item for another. Since most Egyptians were farmers, they exchanged wheat or barley for other goods. They did have copper, gold, and silver for trade. However, they didn't mint it into coins. If they wanted to buy something, they weighed out the metal. During the two centuries before Ptolemaic rule, the Egyptians began minting coins that imitated coins from Athens. They used a gold stater coin to pay Greek mercenaries.

When the Persians conquered Egypt, they banned Greek-style coins in favor of Persian coins. However, most people continued using a barter system or weighing out precious metals. When Alexander the Great arrived, he quickly introduced coins. He had gold and silver drachma coins minted in Egypt, mainly used by the upper-class Egyptians and Greeks.

Most of the working-class Egyptians and Greeks still used a bartering system. However, they now had receipts written on potsherds in either Greek or Egyptian.

Ptolemy I was the first ruler to issue Egypt's own minted coins. Egypt's new money impacted how buying and selling happened. It also promoted the Ptolemaic royal family, whose faces were imprinted on the coins. Egypt had its own copper and gold mines for making coins, but silver had to be imported from Cyprus, Crete, or Persia. Instead of opting out of silver coins, Ptolemy I made them 20 percent smaller, so less silver was needed. As the later Ptolemaic kings faced economic crises, they reduced the amount of gold and silver used in coins even more.

A Ptolemy III gold drachma coin[80]

The Ptolemaic kings quickly banned the use of coins from other countries. Foreign trade conducted in Egypt had to use Egyptian money. Of course, as the kings began using smaller percentages of precious metals in their coins, they profited from exchanging money from countries that used standard amounts of gold and silver in coins.

Ptolemy IV reduced the weight of even the bronze coins. This hurt the working classes, who were paid with bronze coins. Ptolemy V redid the money system with bronze coins in varying amounts. In 53 BCE, Ptolemy XII reduced the silver content in drachma coins to only one-third to pay off his debt to Rome. The last Macedonian ruler, Cleopatra VII, reduced the silver in a drachma by more than half. Supposedly, the reason was for a direct exchange with the Roman denarius.

How did the kingdom's strategic position facilitate trade?

Seas and rivers were the primary trade conduits in the world at that time. The Nile River was Egypt's internal highway. Goods arriving in ports along the Mediterranean Sea could be transported upstream the entire length of the country. If the Nile was swollen and flowing swiftly, sailors had to tow the ships upstream using pack animals or teams of workers from the bank. Fortunately, the prevailing winds usually blew south (and the Nile flows north), so they could sail upstream most of the time. Egypt also used the Nile for trade with Nubia to the south (in today's Sudan).

The Mediterranean was the connection to points near and far. If someone wanted to travel to other places in North Africa, like Libya or Carthage, they usually went by sea rather than risking getting lost in the desert or attacked by fierce Berber tribes. Over a thousand years earlier, the Greeks had established trade colonies around the Mediterranean. Socrates said they were "like frogs around a pond." Early Greek colonies extended as far west as Spain and France.

The Ptolemaic Kingdom sailed its merchant ships around the entire Mediterranean Sea. Ptolemaic coins have even been found in Britain, so the British must have been trade partners. Ptolemaic merchant ships also sailed around the Ionian, Aegean, and Black Seas.

Egypt had yet another water highway. At its eastern border was the Red Sea, which passed along Arabia's shores to the Arabian Sea. From there, ships sailed up the Persian Gulf to Mesopotamia and Persia or south to the Indian Ocean.

The Ptolemaic Kingdom easily accessed the Silk Road's water route from China. Most of East Asia's silk and spice trade did not go overland. Formidable high mountains and lethal deserts lay in the way, overrun with bandits. Typically, the Chinese merchants sailed from the South China Sea to the Indian Ocean and then up the Red Sea. Alternatively, they crossed over the Himalayas to India and then up the Persian Gulf.

Egypt's ships sailed to much of the eastern hemisphere. The trade possibilities were endless.

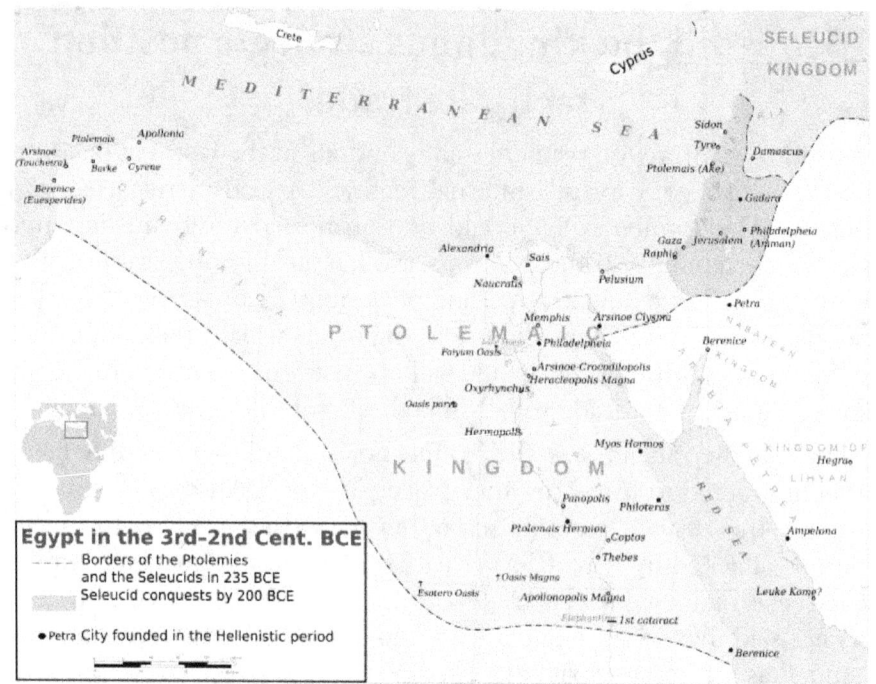

Ptolemaic Kingdom[81]

How did Alexandria and other major ports enhance Egypt's economy?

Alexandria enabled the Ptolemies to expand their overseas influence. The Lighthouse of Alexandria beckoned incoming ships into its secure, double harbor. The harbor also connected the Mediterranean to the Nile.

The Ptolemaic kings multiplied the amount of trade that Egypt had always had. Alexandria was the primary hub, yet the Ptolemies built other new ports or took possession of ports already in existence. Pelusium continued as another Egyptian port on the Mediterranean. However, it began silting over after about a century of Ptolemaic rule. Ptolemy II founded the port of Berenice Troglodytica in southern Egypt, which grew into a prosperous hub on the Red Sea. Ships laden with frankincense crossed the Red Sea from Arabia. Other ships brought silver from the Near East and silk from China. A road with regular watering stations connected the Red Sea port with the port of Coptos on the Nile. Coptos was a strategic port because it was near the Red Sea, and the area was rich in gold and quartz.

About 150 miles south of Coptos was the port of Kom Ombo, also on the Nile. This port was probably where the Ptolemies' war elephants were brought in from Eritrea, near the bottom of the Red Sea. (Eritrean elephants were savanna or bush elephants, the largest living elephants.) The ports in southern Egypt were also a conduit for ivory and gold from central and southern Africa. The Ptolemy Kingdom was famous for its intricately carved ivory furniture and ornaments.

In addition to ports around Egypt, the Ptolemaic Kingdom had the port of Itanos on Crete. It also had ports at Ephesus and Samos in the Aegean Sea. Its ports along West Asia's Mediterranean coast included Nea Paphos and Salamis on Cyprus and Ptolemais in Phoenicia.

Egypt's growing Hellenistic population demanded fine wine. The people's attempts at growing grapevines and producing wine in Egypt were not as successful as they had hoped. Thus, they imported fine wines and ceramics from Crete and Cyprus.

Drawing of Ptolemy IV's Tessarakonteres ship, perhaps the world's largest in its day[32]

Under Ptolemy I, the Ptolemaic Kingdom morphed into the naval powerhouse of the eastern Mediterranean. It could protect its ports and sea highways from nefarious pirates and hostile nations. Naval bases dotting the Aegean and eastern Mediterranean protected the Ptolemaic maritime empire.

Egypt's navy attracted mercenaries from around the Greek world, as the Ptolemies had a reputation for paying the best wages for their navy. In his "Idyll 14," the Greek poet Theocritus mentions this when he writes about a man named Thyonichus meeting his friend Aeschines (paraphrased):

"I'm ill at ease," Aeschines complained.

"Well, that explains why you're thin, your mustache is unkept, and your curls are dry," Thyonichus observed.

"You can joke, but I've been suffering. I'm about to go stark mad."

"You've always been that way, my friend." Thyonichus was unsympathetic. "What's your grievance this time?"

"I was dining with my friends, Apis and Cleonicus, and serving my best wine from Byblos. When we were deep in our cups, we played a drinking game. We each had to name the woman we loved and then drain our cup. So, I named Cynisca. She was sitting right there! We've been together for two months. However, she said nothing! I named her as my true love, and she said nothing! Someone asked her if she'd seen a wolf, and she blushed and answered, 'Shrewdly guessed.' The man beside me whispered, 'A wolf *has* charmed her—the neighbor's tall, handsome son!' If only I could *un*love, Thyonichus! The only cure is to take to the seas. My friend Simus joined a mercenary crew, which cured him of his hopeless love. I, too, shall sail the seas!"

"Well, I hope your love life runs smoothly," Thyonichus said to comfort his friend. "Yet, if you really mean to hire yourself out for someone's navy, Ptolemy II is the best paymaster."

"What else is he?"

"A gentleman. He's witty and has good taste. He's very generous with his money. If you insist on wearing a military cloak and going to war, you should hire yourself to Egypt."[i]

Theocritus's story illustrates the mentality in the Greek world at that time. When a young man encountered seemingly insurmountable issues or wanted a better life, he would hire himself out to one of the Hellenistic armies or navies. The Ptolemaic military offered the best deal. In addition to competitive pay, the Ptolemies gave their military men land grants. They could farm their own land and support a family. Emigrating to Egypt was an attractive option for young men willing to become mercenary soldiers.

---

[i] Theocritus, "Idyll XIV" in *The Project Gutenberg EBook of Theocritus*, https://www.gutenberg.org/files/11533/11533-h/11533-h.htm#IDYLL_XIV.

How was the Ptolemaic economic system organized?

Ptolemaic Egypt's economic chief was the *dioketes*, appointed by the king. He was in charge of establishing and maintaining financial policies. All the ministers of agriculture, finance, and record-keeping answered to him. Egypt had thirty-six provinces called *nomes*. Each nome had an administrator who handled things like currency, land management, and taxes.

The Ptolemaic economy maintained a delicate balance between the Greek monarchy and the Egyptians at the local level. The Greeks introduced agricultural innovations that benefited everyone. However, corruption reared its ugly head, with bureaucrats exploiting their position to enrich themselves. Many of the lower classes ended up in debt to the government because of unfair administrators. It got so bad that when a new Ptolemaic king came to the throne, he magnanimously forgave all debt owed to the Crown so that the victims of corruption could have a clean slate.

The Ptolemaic king owned between one-third to one-half of Egypt's agricultural land, and the temples owned a sizeable slice of the rest. Serfs farmed the land belonging to the Crown and the temples. However, Egypt did have private land ownership, both among the native Egyptians and the Greek military men who received land grants.

Egyptians harvesting papyrus[33]

How did taxes work?

Taxes were the Ptolemaic monarchy's primary income. Usually, landowners paid taxes on their farmland with the grain, fruit, or vegetables they grew. Artisans paid taxes with a percentage of the pottery, fabric, or other goods they produced. The government also taxed each person, taking a regular census to get an accurate count. Each family head had to pay taxes for his wife, children, and any enslaved people.

The Greeks had lower taxes than the Egyptians and other ethnic groups. Greeks living in Alexandria had even lower taxes. Greek schoolteachers and the scholars at the Alexandrian Museum did not have to pay taxes at all. The lower classes of the Egyptians had a reduced tax rate. If farmers owned their land, they got a tax discount on the harvest if they paid for the planting with their own money.

The Ptolemies labeled all priests as "Hellenes," even if they were ethnically Egyptian, so they could get the tax break. The same held true for Egyptian soldiers serving in the Ptolemaic military. Even Egyptian actors and other artists got a tax break if they used their art to promote Hellenistic culture.

What were the key economic activities?

Agriculture was the most significant economic venture. Greece lacked enough arable land to feed its population, so Egypt shipped grain there. Also, it increasingly supplied Rome's need for grain, especially in the Ptolemaic Kingdom's last century. Papyrus reeds were native to Egypt's wetlands, especially the Delta, and were used to make paper, which became another export. Egypt also shipped out luxury items like dyed cloth, jewelry, and artwork.

Egypt was well-known for manufacturing glassware. Egyptian faience was a vivid blue or green transparent glass used for jewelry or as a glaze on pottery. Items made with faience became a notable export.

A Ptolemaic-er falcon with faience glaze[34]

The Egyptians preferred wearing thin, comfortable linen, but the Greeks liked wool. Thus, the Ptolemies increased herds of sheep and goats to produce clothing, rugs, and tapestries. They were woven with brightly dyed wool into patterns reflecting an exciting fusion of Egyptian and Greek designs.

Egypt had always been a significant manufacturer of perfumes, cosmetics, and medicine. It had natural resources, like natron for soap and antiseptics and malachite for eye makeup.

What were the economic policies of the early Ptolemies?

Ptolemy I avoided jumping into wars that wasted manpower and money without positive economic outcomes for Egypt. Instead, he invested his people and resources into building a better and stronger Egypt. When Ptolemy I inserted himself into the Wars of the Diadochi, his main objective was gaining control of the coastal regions of Syria, Phoenicia, and Judea, which had a two-pronged benefit. For one thing, they acted as a buffer zone for Egypt. A protected and secure Egypt was a more prosperous Egypt. Secondly, controlling West Asia's coast meant controlling its fantastically wealthy trade, giving Egypt the upper hand economically.

Ptolemy II's completion of the Lighthouse of Alexandria increased ship traffic into Alexandria, and his economic endeavors expanded tax revenue. J. G. Manning, a history professor at Yale University, believes Ptolemy II was the wealthiest person in the world in his day.[1]

Unfortunately, Ptolemaic Egypt could not sustain the peak of wealth it enjoyed in its first century. Climate change caused cooler weather some years, leading to less rainfall at the Nile sources. Decimated agricultural output meant Egypt had trouble feeding its people, much less shipping grain to Greece and Rome. The devaluation of coins created issues with international trade, and the cost of wars emptied the treasury. Nevertheless, despite all its woes and depleted wealth, Ptolemaic Egypt maintained one of the world's most significant economies until it fell to Rome.

---

[1] J. G. Manning, *Land and Power in Ptolemaic Egypt* (Cambridge University Press, 2007), 129.

Chapter 7: The Ptolemaic Wars and Strategies for Survival

The cornerstone of the Ptolemaic state was its military. The army was the engine that drove the Ptolemies' expansion efforts, blended Greeks and Egyptians into one unit, defended Egypt from attack, and protected it from internal uprisings. "The Ptolemaic Army … was at all times a military body structured for armed conflict, a colonizing and occupying presence mainly in Egypt, and a reflection and auxiliary of the monarchic project of the Ptolemies themselves."[i]

The Ptolemies' Hellenistic culture influenced them to establish a highly organized, disciplined, and well-equipped force. The Ptolemaic dynasty not only survived longer than the other Hellenistic kingdoms, but thrived. What strategies and conflicts defined the Ptolemaic Kingdom's efforts to maintain and expand power? How did their recruiting system and military innovations defend the kingdom? This chapter will look at these topics in more detail.

Who served in the Ptolemaic military?

The soldiers serving in the Ptolemaic army, both Greek and Egyptian, were privileged people. They got tax breaks and free land, and the higher status of the military provided incentives to join.

---

[i] Paul A. Johstono, *The Army of Ptolemaic Egypt 323-204 BC: An Institutional and Operational History* (Pen & Sword Military, 2020).

Ancient Egypt did not always have a standing army. The farmers were also the infantry, so Egypt went to war when its people were not in the middle of planting or harvesting. However, the Ptolemaic royal army had permanent units that always stood ready to mobilize.

Mosaic of Ptolemaic Egypt's Greek soldiers³⁵

The army included soldiers with a proud heritage, the descendants of the men who fought with Alexander the Great. It also included Greeks who immigrated to Egypt by the thousands. They saw Egypt as a bright, Hellenistic land full of opportunities. They were masters of Greek weaponry and the phalanx formation, which the Ptolemies continued using.

Beginning with Ptolemy II, native Egyptians flooded into the army. As we've mentioned, the Ptolemies carefully portrayed themselves not as conquerors but as a continuation of the ancient pharaohs. As one scholar writes, "The 'marriage' between army and temple, incorporating Greeks, Greco-Egyptians, and Egyptians, became one of the pillars of Ptolemaic power and survival in the latter part of the Hellenistic era."ⁱ

Some of the Ptolemaic army's professional, full-time soldiers were mercenaries from other countries who lived in Egypt year-round. If no wars were going on, they manned the forts and garrisons around the country, spending their time in training. The next and largest group were military settlers. They had farms and families but served in the military regularly in the off-season for agriculture. The government gave them

---

ⁱ Hans Hauben, "Review of 'Army and Society in Ptolemaic Egypt: From Invasion to Integration,' by Christelle Fischer-Bovet," *The Bulletin of the American Society of Papyrologists* 53 (2016): 395-409, http://www.jstor.org/stable/44968458.

land allotments called *klerouchoi* (cleruchs). The Egyptian soldiers got about ten acres, and the Greeks got fifteen. Allotments for cavalry riders (of any ethnicity) went up to fifty acres, and officers usually got more. The last group was foreign mercenaries who did not live in Egypt but signed on to fight in a specific war. They received a generous salary but no other benefits.

How were new soldiers recruited?

The Ptolemaic kings had *xenologoi*, army recruiters who went abroad to enlist new soldiers, most of whom were volunteers. Most recruits were Greek, but the recruiters also hired soldiers from North Africa, Arabia, and Syria. Celtic-speaking tribes, including the Galatians, flooded into Macedonia, Thrace, and the Black Sea region in the Ptolemaic era. They were fierce fighters without particular allegiance to anyone, making them ideal mercenaries. Cavalry recruits mostly came from Anatolia, Judea, Persia, and Thrace.

Another source of recruits were prisoners of war, such as those brought by Ptolemy I into Egypt from Judea and Gaza. Despite not being voluntary soldiers, they still got plots of land.

How was the military organized?

The king was the top military leader. After consulting with his generals and advisors, he decided when and where to go to war. He was expected to lead his men into battle and fight with them. Following the tradition of Alexander the Great, the king usually led the elite cavalry forces. He had the flexibility to move around the battlefield and direct cavalry or infantry to areas needing assistance.

Directly under the king were the generals, called *strategoi*. Some generals served as governors of the Ptolemaic provinces, which meant they were there if war broke out in the region. The infantry formed units of about one thousand men, called *chiliarchies*, led by a commander called a *hegemon*. The *máchimoi* were native Egyptian soldiers. The Greek historian Herodotus said they were a particular caste in Egypt (predating the Ptolemaic and Persian rule). Under Ptolemaic rule, they served as guards, police, and military.

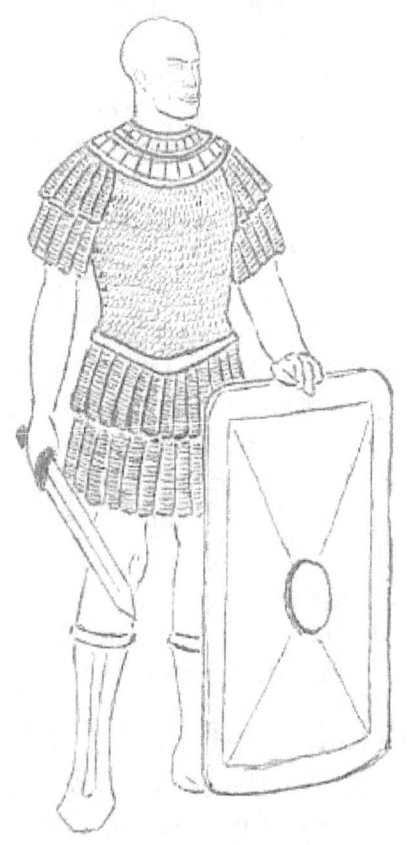

An Egyptian máchimos[86]

The cavalry formed units of around five hundred horseback riders called *hipparchies*. The cavalry unit commander was a *hipparch* with a status similar to a hegemon. The Ptolemaic army had elite units, such as the *agema*, with three thousand cavalry and *hypaspist* infantry. The hypaspist infantry were a legacy of Alexander the Great and his father, Philip II. They were chosen from the working class for their determination, ability, and fast movement. Their armor and weaponry were lightweight, giving them speed and agility for lightning-fast strikes or fighting on rough terrain.

Another elite unit was the royal guard surrounding the king. Among them were his bodyguards, who were also his military advisors. The royal guard had seven hundred heavy cavalry stationed in Alexandria when not at war. Heavy cavalry used large warhorses with body armor, like breastplates. The riders carried heavy swords, lances, and battle axes.

The heavy cavalry typically engaged in shock charges, mowing down the opponents and smashing them with the heavy weaponry.

The Ptolemaic kings were proud of their herd of war elephants, meant to shock and awe. However, the African breed they used did not work out well in battle, as discussed later in the chapter. Eventually, they gave up on using elephants in war.

What about the navy?

Ptolemy I focused on building an exceptional navy while the other Diadochi fought over Greece, Macedonia, and Asia. The two primary naval bases were at Cyprus and Alexandria. Ptolemy commanded his navy in person and initially was the dominant force in the eastern Mediterranean. In 306 BCE, disaster struck when he suffered a brutal loss off the coast of Salamis, Cyprus.

Ptolemy I had earlier taken control of Cyprus. He put his brother, Menelaus, in charge of the island. He used it as his base for attacking Antigonus I in Syria and Turkey. Antigonus sent his son Demetrius to neutralize Cyprus as a Ptolemaic operations center. Demetrius landed in Cyprus, marched overland, and met Menelaus in battle five miles out of Salamis. Menelaus lost the first clash, then hunkered down in Salamis while desperately messaging Ptolemy for help. He nervously waited as Demetrius began building deadly siege engines: massive battering rams, catapults, and a siege tower on wheels that was 150 feet high.

In a ferocious attack, Demetrius smashed part of Salamis's wall. However, Menelaus's men snuck out by night and burned Demetrius's siege engines, buying the city some time. Meanwhile, Ptolemy was sailing to his brother's rescue from Alexandria. He had 140 warships and 200 transport ships carrying 10,000 troops. Demetrius had at least 180 ships, which he had not yet used in his invasion. He had 15,000 soldiers and 500 cavalry surrounding Salamis.

Ptolemy I messaged Demetrius, "Leave Cyprus now!"

Demetrius replied, "I will leave if you remove your garrisons from Corinth and Sicyon in Greece."

Ptolemy snorted at this, then sailed around the island by night, hoping to launch a sneak attack offshore of Salamis, where his brother had sixty ships. Yet, Demetrius was one step ahead of him. Guessing what Ptolemy would do, he armed his ships with missile throwers and stationed them outside Salamis's harbor. At dawn, Ptolemy sailed in to see Demetrius's fleet floating between him and Salamis.

Demetrius left ten of his ships at the harbor's narrow entrance, blocking Menelaus from deploying his ships. He sailed the rest of his fleet out to meet Ptolemy. The two navies bore down on each other, using their battering rams to smash the enemy ships. Sometimes, the ram impaled the side of another vessel, holding the two boats together, and the men jumped aboard to fight hand-to-hand. Another trick was sailing just next to another ship, shearing off its oars and leaving it dead in the water. The two forces sent hails of arrows and javelins at their opponents. They flung rocks with their *ballistae*, catapults with levers powered by torsion springs.

Ballista[37]

Ptolemy's men were able to board Demetrius's ship, killing or severely wounding his bodyguards. Nevertheless, Demetrius fought like a tiger, throwing missiles and spearing anyone who got close. Projectiles hit him, but his armor protected him. Demetrius and his men finally forced Ptolemy's troops off the ship. The sea battle raged on as Demetrius shattered the right wing of Ptolemy's navy. From his position on the left wing, Ptolemy saw a horrifying sight. His ships on the far right were sinking, and his vessels in the middle were sailing away from the battle. Ptolemy had no choice but to swing around and follow the rest of his ships in flight.[i]

It took Ptolemy I ten years to rebuild his navy and retake Cyprus. Ptolemy II fought and lost several battles in the Aegean Sea. Eventually, military activities shifted from sea battles to land battles in Syria and Egypt. The navy had become defunct by the beginning of Ptolemy V's reign.

Why was Antigonus's attempt to annex Egypt an abject failure?

Inspired by Demetrius's naval victory, his father, Antigonus I, decided he could take Egypt with a dual assault by land and sea. In the winter of 306 BCE, Antigonus marched on Egypt while Demetrius sailed his navy to Alexandria. In this attack, Ptolemy discovered a new advantage of having Alexandria in the Nile Delta as his capital. The Delta was swampland with several branches of the Nile barring the way from an army arriving from West Asia. It was too boggy for Antigonus's land army, not to mention the logistics of crossing multiple rivers.

Getting provisions for the land army was a nightmare. Antigonus had depended on Demetrius to deliver supplies by sea. However, storms kept Demetrius from arriving at the expected time. When his navy finally arrived at Alexandria, Demetrius faced unexpected resistance. Ptolemy held him off, thanks to his harbor design. Meanwhile, Antigonus's army was starving and had to abandon the expedition as Demetrius sailed away from Africa's coast.

Alexandria's Ingenious Harbor

Alexandria's primary harbor was the island of Pharos. The secondary harbor was the peninsula jutting out from the mainland to the east of Pharos, where the palace was. Ships also moored in the freshwater Lake Mareotis just south of Alexandria's walls, which connected to the Nile via canals. Alexandria's challenge with ship traffic was offshore waves and wind that abruptly changed directions. If the waves or wind from the east were too disruptive, the ships could move to the secondary harbor,

---

[i] Diodorus, *Library of History*, Volume X.

where the peninsula protected them, or to Lake Mareotis.

The Heptastadion causeway from the city to Pharos Island enabled foot and cart traffic from the harbor to the city. It also offered protection from wind and waves from the west. When designing the Heptastadion, Dinocrates ingeniously placed several canals through which ships could pass. If Alexandria was under attack by sea, it enabled the vessels in the harbor to move around to safety. It also meant that the military could post catapults and archers on Pharos and the causeways, launching missiles at attacking ships and preventing access to the mainland.

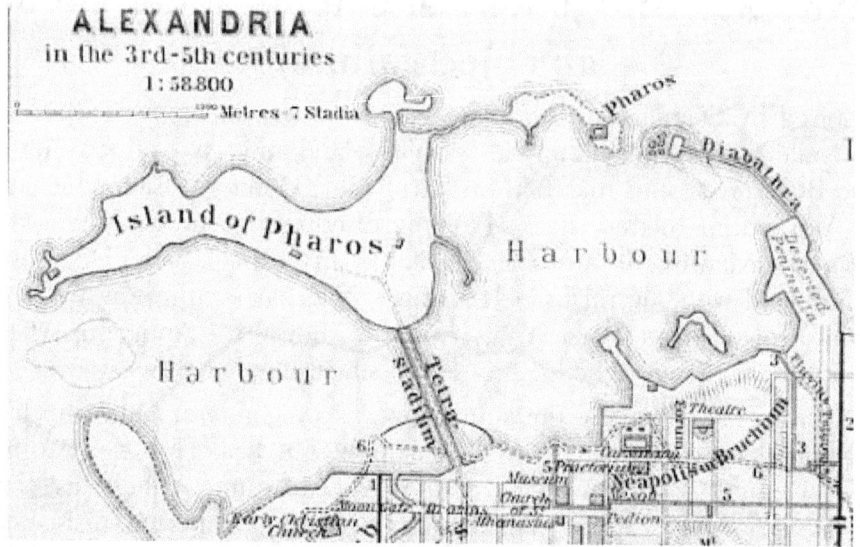

Alexandria's Harbor[38]

The Great Battle of Rafia on the Border of the Sinai and Gaza Strip

In 217 BCE, one of history's most extensive land battles raged between the Sinai Desert and Gaza. It was the final clash of the Fourth Syrian War. Ptolemy IV had about seventy-five thousand men, and Antiochus III had nearly as many. Their troops faced off, with the front lines extending for miles. The Greek general Polybius wrote a detailed account of the great clash between the Titans. His report opens a window into the Ptolemaic army's organization, command units, divisions, and battle tactics.

Ptolemy IV commanded his left wing, which had Egypt's elite forces. Seven hundred of his three thousand cavalry were his highly trained palace guards, and the rest were Libyan and Egyptian horseback riders. Forty African war elephants bellowed and stomped as they waited for the battle to begin. He had three thousand light infantry from Crete and five thousand infantrymen. Of these, two thousand were Thracian *peltastai*, skirmishers who carried crescent-shaped shields, javelins, and swords. The rest were the *agema*, the royal squadron that surrounded the king.

A peltast infantryman with his crescent shield[39]

On the right wing of Ptolemy IV's army were six thousand more foot soldiers from Galatia and Thrace, thirty-three more war elephants, two thousand Greek cavalry, and more mercenaries. The regular infantry lined up in a phalanx position in the center of the Ptolemaic army. It numbered twenty thousand Egyptians, eight thousand Greek mercenaries, twenty-five thousand Macedonians, and three thousand Libyans. The Greeks developed the rigid discipline of the phalanx position, with the foot soldiers forming rows where they stood shoulder to shoulder. Their shields overlapped slightly, and long spears extended from the front row. The soldiers behind the first row held their shields over their heads, forming a ceiling of shields. The arrows shot by the enemy simply bounced off. If an infantryman on the front line fell, the man behind him stepped into his place.

The phalanx had been the core of Alexander's army, and the Ptolemies continued the tradition. The Macedonian phalanx usually had sixteen soldiers in a row, yet it was flexible. Depending on the terrain or how the opposing army lined up, it could have as few as eight in a row or up to thirty-two. The shorter lines worked well for quick mobility if the phalanx had to move to the side quickly in situations like an elephant or scythed chariot charging them.

As mentioned earlier, Ptolemy IV was guilty of ignoring matters in Egypt while indulging his every whim. He had left his corrupt advisors, Sosibius and Agathocles, to deal with the government. The Seleucid king, Antiochus III, took advantage of Ptolemy's inattention to invade Syria and Phoenicia. Egypt's naval commander, Theodotus, defected to Antiochus, bringing part of Ptolemy's navy with him. Ptolemy IV had not been recruiting new soldiers or properly equipping his army. They were in no shape to fight the Seleucids.

Ptolemy IV had no idea what to do, but his advisors rose to the occasion. Sosibius reached out to Antiochus, who agreed to a temporary ceasefire. They convinced Antiochus that Ptolemy had no interest in fighting and wanted to discuss peace terms, using nearby governors as intermediaries. While the negotiators traveled back and forth from Egypt to Syria for months, the Ptolemaic Kingdom briskly prepared for war. It sent out recruiters for Greek mercenaries, stockpiled supplies, and trained its men. The recruiting efforts went splendidly, bringing in nearly twenty thousand soldiers from abroad.

The kingdom also recruited two stellar leaders. Polycrates of Argos, the governor of Cyprus, drilled the troops, pumping them full of enthusiasm. In the Battle of Raphia, he rode with Ptolemy IV in the left wing, commanding the cavalry. Andromachus of Aspendus drilled the infantry in the phalanx maneuvers and led them into battle.

Meanwhile, Antiochus III continued in his delusion that Egypt did not want war. Winter was approaching, so he left Syria for his winter quarters in Seleucia. He did not even bother to drill his troops during the winter months. Negotiations for a settlement dragged on through the winter while Ptolemy's crew whipped his army into shape.

When spring arrived, it finally dawned on Antiochus that Ptolemy IV intended to take Syria back. He heard that Ptolemy had rallied his men at Alexandria and was marching toward Gaza. Ptolemy and his sister-wife, Arsinoe III, rode their horses along their front lines, calling the troops to arms. Ptolemy IV had no glorious achievements of his own to fire up the troops, so he tried to inspire them with what their ancestors had done. He also promised extraordinary rewards if Egypt won the battle.

Meanwhile, Antiochus rallied his troops and marched south. He also had his Macedonian-style phalanx in the center with mercenaries from Greece and Crete. He had sixty elephants on his right wing, directly across from Ptolemy IV's elephants. Behind the elephants and angling off were four thousand cavalry. He had another two thousand cavalry on his left wing, with javelin throwers, three thousand light infantry, and the rest of his elephants. His Arab troops were between the cavalry and the phalanx.

War elephants[40]

The two armies collided at Raphia, at the border of Gaza. The battle began with an elephant charge from both sides, which was cringeworthy for Ptolemy IV. Most of his elephants refused to fight. The remaining elephants crashed into the opposing elephants' foreheads, locking tusks. It was then a battle of strength, with each massive creature trying to wrestle the other to the ground or turn them around. If one elephant could swipe another's trunk so it turned around, the stronger elephant would gore the other in the rear end. Each elephant had a tower on its back where men with spears rode. As the elephants wrestled, the spearmen tried to impale the enemy spearmen on the other elephants.

The problem for Ptolemy IV was that he had African elephants. They were bigger and more aggressive than the Indian elephants used by Antiochus. However, they could not stand the smell of the Indian elephants, which is why most of them turned and rushed off the battleground. While this fiasco played out, the Seleucid cavalry charged the Ptolemaic cavalry led by Polycrates. On the other end of the line, the elephants threw Ptolemy's Thracian infantry into disarray. Ptolemy's entire left wing was in retreat.

However, Echecrates, a commander in Ptolemy IV's right wing, saw the left wing falling apart. He ordered the Greek mercenaries to attack the enemy on their left wing. At the same time, he led the cavalry in a charge, flanked the enemy elephants, and chased off the enemy cavalry.

Ptolemy IV's phalanx stood nervously in the middle, uncertain what to do. Suddenly, Ptolemy raced just ahead of their front lines, leading them in a charge. They lowered their spears, and the opposing infantry fled the field.

Meanwhile, Antiochus thought he had won the day after his elephants crashed through Ptolemy's troops. He was chasing down a few stragglers when he realized most of his army was racing off the battlefield, with Ptolemy's men in hot pursuit.

Night was falling, so both sides retreated to their camps. The next morning, they buried their dead. At first, Antiochus planned to face off for battle again. He did not realize how dreadful things were. Most of Antiochus's surviving men had hidden in Gaza, so he had to round them up. When he began burying his men, he discovered he had lost 13,000. Ptolemy IV had captured another 4,000. Ptolemy lost 2,200 men and most of his elephants.

Antiochus offered the rites of honor over his dead soldiers, then rounded up the living ones and returned to Seleucia. Ptolemy IV took back Gaza, Syria, and Phoenicia. His victory astonished his citizens, who were unaccustomed to their king accomplishing anything.[i] The momentous battle temporarily arrested the Ptolemaic Kingdom's downward spiral.

---

[i] Polybius, *The Histories* (Loeb Classical Library Edition, 1923), Book V, https://penelope.uchicago.edu/Thaer/E/Roman/Texts/Polybius/5*.html.

Polybius believed that when the native Egyptians mobilized en masse at the Battle of Raphia, it awakened them to a new reality. They now held sway! Before Raphia, the Egyptians only comprised a fraction of the Ptolemaic military. Now, they played a vital role. This self-awareness simmered for about a decade as they considered what they could do with their newly realized power.

Beginning with Ptolemy V, internal struggle derailed Egypt's military operations outside the country. The royal family spent more time fighting each other than fighting outside threats like Rome, and uprisings and civil war rocked the kingdom.

Chapter 8: Decline and Fall of Ptolemaic Rule

What led to the weakening and eventual collapse of the Ptolemaic Kingdom? It involved internal issues like civil wars and the treasury going bankrupt. External threats, like Egypt's conflict with rival Hellenistic states, led Rome to insert itself. However, the ultimate death blow came from a string of weak rulers and the loss of centralized control. This chapter unwraps how it all played out.

The Rising Threat of Rome

When Ptolemy I became Egypt's king, Rome was a modest republic ruling central Italy. However, during Ptolemy II's reign, Rome began attacking the ancient Greek colonies in southern Italy. King Pyrrhus of Epirus (northwestern Greece) sailed to the rescue. Ptolemy sent twenty war elephants to help drive the Romans out of southern Italy. Pyrrhus initially won two costly "Pyrrhic" victories. Nevertheless, he lost the war, and Rome took southern Italy. Oddly, Ptolemy II sent an embassy to Rome two years later with gifts, pledging friendship.[i]

It was not long before Rome launched its first offshore war in Sicily, which meant it had to build a navy. Despite never before fighting at sea, Rome trounced Carthage in the world's largest naval battle. Rome won

---

[i] Mary Siani-Davies, "Ptolemy XII Auletes and the Romans," *Historia: Zeitschrift Für Alte Geschichte* 46, no. 3 (1997): 308. http://www.jstor.org/stable/4436474.

Sicily in 241 BCE, during Ptolemy III's reign. Rome continued its empire building in Ptolemy IV's reign, capturing Spain and destroying Carthage in North Africa. The legendary sea empire had to give up its navy and pay tribute to Rome.

When Ptolemy V was ruling Egypt, Rome began attacking Greece and Macedonia. Inconceivably, the Ptolemaic leaders seemed oblivious to the threat Rome presented. It never seemed to dawn on them that Rome might one day attack Egypt. Instead, the Ptolemaic royal family regarded Rome as the playground nanny. They ran to the Roman Senate with their dynastic disputes, asking for arbitration. In so doing, they ultimately gave Rome a foothold.

Ptolemy VI Philometor⁴¹

A Tale of Two Brothers: Ptolemy VI Philometor and Ptolemy VIII Physcon

When Ptolemy V dropped dead at age thirty, his oldest son by his queen and co-ruler, Cleopatra Syra ("the Syrian," daughter of Antiochus III the Great, ruler of the Seleucid Empire), was Ptolemy VI Philometor. He was only six years old. Ptolemy VI ascended the throne in 180 BCE, with his mother as his regent.

Cleopatra Syra became the first queen of the Ptolemaic Kingdom to rule when her husband was not living. Ptolemy V had been preparing to invade the Seleucid Empire, but his death cut those plans short. Cleopatra's first act as queen regent was to call off the war against her homeland. She did not want to fight her brother, Seleucus IV, now the ruler of the Seleucid Empire. Three years later, Cleopatra suddenly died.

"She was young!" people whispered. "Not even thirty yet."

"Do you think she was poisoned?" others wondered.

"Who will be the boy king's regent now?"

"She named Lenaeus and the eunuch Eulaeus as co-regents on her deathbed."

"Who are they?"

"Nobody! They're not Greek—they're barbarians.[1] Both were slaves. They came with Cleopatra Syra to Egypt. Eulaeus is Ptolemy VI's tutor."

"They must be the only ones she trusted."

Eulaeus and Lenaeus knew they had to declare Ptolemy VI an adult quickly. Otherwise, Rome would insert itself into Egyptian politics. Ptolemy VI celebrated his *anaklētēria* or coming-of-age ceremony in 172 BCE when he was fourteen. Two years later, he married his sister, Cleopatra II, making her his co-ruler. Eulaeus and Lenaeus still ran things as advisors.

By this time, Ptolemy VI's uncle, Antiochus IV Epiphanes, had seized the Seleucid throne at his brother's death. Eccentric and unhinged, he refused Ptolemy VI's demand to return Coele-Syria to Egypt. Coele-Syria, which included Judea, was Cleopatra Syra's dowry when she married Ptolemy V. Eulaeus and Lenaeus sent an army to Syria. However, before it reached Gaza, Antiochus Epiphanes charged south and crushed the army in the Sinai Desert.

Antiochus crossed the Sinai and marched into Egypt, capturing Pelusium and then Memphis. This was the first foreign invasion of Egypt since Antigonus I's failed attempt over a century earlier. Ptolemy VI tried to sail out of Alexandria to safety, but his uncle Antiochus captured him, taking him prisoner.

Antiochus Epiphanes had himself crowned king by Egypt's priests. He loved play-acting and was well-known for strange and unconventional behavior. This "crowning" seems to have been an absurd joke, not to be taken seriously.

The Greeks in Alexandria tired of rule by foreign regents while Antiochus held their king captive. They staged a revolt in 170 BCE, overthrowing Eulaeus and Lenaeus. Since Ptolemy VI was still his uncle's prisoner in Memphis, they made his younger brother, Ptolemy VIII, the next king. His nickname was "Physcon," or "fatty." Why did

---

[1] For the ancient Greeks, the word βάρβαροι (barbaroi) meant "babbler," or people who spoke a language that was not Greek. It was a catch-all label for non-Greek people.

they jump from Ptolemy VI to Ptolemy VIII? Who was Ptolemy VII, and what happened to him? He was apparently a son of Ptolemy VI who may have briefly ruled (as a small child) before being murdered by his uncle, Ptolemy VIII Physcon.

Ptolemy VIII was only fourteen when he took his older brother's place in Alexandria. Antiochus Epiphanes still held Memphis and the eastern Delta for another year. However, he returned to Syria in 169 BCE, leaving Ptolemy VI as king of Memphis. Egypt was divided between two brothers. However, their sister, Cleopatra II (Ptolemy VI's wife), negotiated an agreement where all three would rule together.

Ptolemy VI and Cleopatra II[48]

This plan enraged Antiochus Epiphanes, who wanted Egypt divided and weak. He invaded Egypt again, stopping off in Jerusalem on his way. Antiochus had been imposing Hellenistic culture and religion on the Seleucid Empire. His predecessors promoted Greek ways while respecting the culture and religion of their conquered people. Yet, Antiochus Epiphanes harbored nothing but disrespect for the Jews. They had adopted some Hellenistic ways, but they insisted on worshiping their one god and no one else. Antiochus appointed a Hellenistic Jew named Menelaus as Jerusalem's new high priest. Menelaus was willing to syncretize Judaism with the Greek gods. Antiochus helped himself to the temple treasure to pay for his war and headed to Egypt in 168 BCE.

Antiochus Epiphanes retook Memphis, and his next target was Alexandria. At this point, Rome got involved, pretending to be a negotiator. Their motive was to prevent the spread of the Seleucid Empire. As Antiochus Epiphanes approached Alexandria, the Roman proconsul, Popillius, intercepted him:

"I have orders from the Roman Senate. Leave Egypt at once or face war with Rome."

Antiochus stared in stunned shock as the elderly envoy drew a circle around him in the sand. "Stay there in that circle until you give me an answer for the Senate!"

Trembling in humiliation and rage, Antiochus left Egypt. He had to go through Judea on his way back to Syria. His fury knew no bounds when he found out that the Jews had reinstalled their former priest in the temple. Antiochus Epiphanes launched a three-day killing spree, massacring forty thousand Jews, including women and children. He outlawed Judaism, put Zeus's statue in the Jewish temple, and slaughtered a pig on its altar. These outrages spawned the Maccabean Revolt, in which the Jews won independence from the Seleucid Empire. Their new state provided a buffer zone between Egypt and Syria.

For the next five years, Ptolemy VI and VIII ruled with their sister, Cleopatra II. Ptolemy VI Philometor was gentle and accommodating, happy to coexist with his younger brother. Yet, Ptolemy VIII Physcon's unbridled ambition got in the way. His friend, Dionysius Petosarapis, convinced him to launch a mob on Philometor's palace to kill him. The plot fell through, and Philometor gave Physcon the option to abdicate.

Ptolemy VIII Physcon[48]

Physcon tried to convince his older brother of his innocence. "My brother! I knew nothing about this uprising. I swear!"

Philometor believed him, and the two appeared together before the people on the palace portico.

Dionysius realized he needed to get out of town fast. He swam naked across the Nile and hid among the native Egyptians, plotting a renewed revolt. In 164 BCE, the rebels forced Ptolemy VI Philometor to flee to Rome, ending the five years of double kingship.

When Philometor presented his case to the Roman Senate (still masquerading as arbitrators), it played right into their hands. Just like Antiochus Epiphanes, they wanted a divided and weaker Egypt. They proposed dividing the Ptolemaic Kingdom. Ptolemy VI Philometor would get Egypt and Cyprus, and Ptolemy VIII Physcon would get Cyrene. Philometor sailed to Cyprus to await Rome's negotiations with his brother. However, in Philometor's absence from Egypt, Physcon became a ferocious tyrant, inciting an uproar. If the Romans had not intervened, Egypt's people would have torn Physcon limb from limb. They begged Philometor to return, which he did, as Physcon sailed off to Cyrene in 163 BCE.

For the rest of his life, Ptolemy VI Philometor and his queen, Cleopatra II, were Egypt's only rulers. However, Ptolemy VIII Physcon was still stirring up trouble. He visited Rome and complained to the Senate: "It isn't fair! You gave Egypt *and* Cyprus to Philometor. All I got was Cyrene."

The Senate agreed that Physcon should also have Cyprus. When the Roman envoys traveled to Egypt to convince Philometor to concede Cyprus, he refused. Rome let the matter drop, and Cyprus remained in Philometor's hands.

In 146 BCE, Ptolemy VI invaded Syria. The Jews allowed his army to pass through Judea on his way. Ptolemy VI conquered all the coastal cities belonging to the Seleucid Empire, and the leaders of Antioch crowned him Asia's king. However, Ptolemy VI worried that Rome would interfere if he snatched the entire Seleucid Empire. He kept Syria, once part of the Ptolemaic Kingdom. Shortly before returning to Egypt, he fell from his horse, fracturing his skull, and died five days later.

Ptolemy VI's teenage son had recently died, and his only other son was seven. The door was open for Ptolemy VIII to take back Egypt. He had maintained friendly relations with the Roman Senate. Confident they had his back, he sailed to Egypt in 145 BCE. He married his sister and Ptolemy VI's widow, Cleopatra II. She gave birth to their only child, Ptolemy Memphites, in 143 BCE. Ptolemy VIII viciously purged everyone who had supported Ptolemy VI over him.

While still married to Cleopatra II, he married her daughter by Ptolemy VI, Cleopatra III. An infuriated Cleopatra II initiated an uprising. After the Alexandrians set fire to the palace, Ptolemy VIII escaped to Cyprus with Cleopatra III. A native Egyptian named Harsiesi took advantage of the chaos to generate a rebellion in southern Egypt and take control. Eventually, Ptolemy VIII and Cleopatra III returned to Egypt with their children and settled in Memphis in 130 BCE. His forces were able to kill Harsiesi and reunite Egypt.

Ptolemy VIII killed Memphites, his son by Cleopatra II, chopped him up, and sent the body parts to the boy's mother on her birthday. Cleopatra II grabbed the royal treasury and sailed to Syria, where Demetrius II was ruler of the Seleucid Empire. His wife was her daughter, Cleopatra Thea. However, inexplicably, Cleopatra II returned to Egypt and reconciled with her second husband and brother in 124 BCE. They co-ruled until Ptolemy VIII died in 116 BCE.

Ptolemy IX"

Ptolemy IX Soter and Ptolemy X Alexander I Continue the Messy Family Politics (116-81 BCE)

When Ptolemy VIII died, his son, Ptolemy IX Soter, became king. He co-ruled with his grandmother, Cleopatra II, and his mother, Cleopatra III. Cleopatra II died the following year after sixty years as Egypt's queen. Before becoming king, Ptolemy IX had married his full sister, Cleopatra IV, and they had two children together. However, after Cleopatra II died and Cleopatra III gained more power, she forced her son to divorce Cleopatra IV. Apparently, the mother and daughter had fallen out. She had Ptolemy IX marry his other sister, Cleopatra Selene.

Ptolemy IX followed his mother's orders, but tensions grew between mother and son. Cleopatra IV sailed to Cyprus, where her younger brother, Ptolemy X, was governor. She married her cousin, Antiochus IX, ruler of the Seleucid Empire. In Egypt, Ptolemy IX and Cleopatra Selene had a daughter named Berenice III in 114 BCE.

Finally, the unpredictable Cleopatra III ejected Ptolemy IX from Egypt in 107 BCE, forcing him to divorce Cleopatra Selene. Cleopatra III made her younger son, Ptolemy X, the next king and had him marry Cleopatra Selene. In exile, Ptolemy IX took control of Cyprus.

Ptolemy X and his mother allied with Antiochus VIII Grypus, son of Cleopatra Thea and Demetrius II. Grypus was fighting his half-brother, Antiochus IX Cyzicenus, for control of the Seleucid Empire. Cleopatra III forced Ptolemy X and Cleopatra Selene to divorce as part of the deal. Why? Cleopatra Selene now had to marry her third husband, her cousin

Antiochus VIII. By 101 BCE, Ptolemy X's anger finally boiled over at his mother's mechanisms, and he arranged her murder.

Berenice III, a Strong-Willed and Beloved Queen (101–88, 81–80 BCE)

After killing his mother, Ptolemy X married his thirteen-year-old niece, Berenice, the daughter of his brother, Ptolemy IX, and sister, Cleopatra Selene. Berenice became his co-ruler. By this time, he was a hopeless drunk and so fat he could not walk without his servants holding him up. Ptolemy X had to deal with the uprisings of native Egyptians in 91 BCE. They took control of Thebes and cut off Ptolemy X's interactions with Nubia.

Berenice III[46]

The citizens of Alexandria became increasingly dissatisfied with Ptolemy X's botched attempts at running the country. His army staged a coup, forcing him and Berenice out of Egypt in 88 BCE. They then recalled Ptolemy IX to be their king again. Ptolemy X raised a mercenary army in Syria and got his throne back. However, needing money to pay his soldiers, he raided Alexander the Great's tomb and melted down his gold coffin. The Greeks were appalled at this dreadful sacrilege. His scandalized subjects drove Ptolemy X out of the country again, and he died in a naval battle off Cyprus.

Now a widow, Berenice returned to Egypt, where her father, Ptolemy IX, was king again. He made Berenice his co-regent, and some sources say he married her. His death a few months later left Berenice as Egypt's first female ruler without being the wife or mother of a king. Her subjects thought she was a model queen. She properly worshiped the Greek and Egyptian gods, was unpretentious, and respected the growing Jewish population (now about 25 percent of Alexandria's population).

Her subjects loved Berenice but felt she should be married. Berenice knew she needed to stabilize her shaky throne, but who would she marry? The Roman dictator Sulla suggested that she marry Ptolemy XI Alexander. He was Berenice's half-brother, as Cleopatra Serene was their mother. His father was Ptolemy X, so Berenice had also been his stepmother. Ptolemy XI was the only living legitimate male of the Ptolemaic family.

The marriage lasted only nineteen days. Ptolemy XI murdered Berenice, perhaps angry that she did not make him the full king of the Ptolemaic Kingdom. The horrified Alexandrians chased him into the gymnasium and killed him, leaving Egypt with no ruler.

Ptolemy XII Auletes, the Illegitimate Son (80–58, 55–51 BCE)

The Ptolemy family had run out of legitimate offspring. Who would become the next ruler? Ptolemy XII Auletes, Ptolemy IX's son by a non-royal mother, became king. He married his relative, Cleopatra V, making her co-regent. They had five children, but their second-oldest daughter, Cleopatra VII, was the famous Cleopatra who got involved in sultry affairs with Julius Caesar and Mark Antony.

Ptolemy XII immediately faced multiple challenges. Egypt was plunging into decline, and its relations with Rome were precarious. In 75 BCE, Rome grabbed Cyrene, a major grain producer, which had been part of the Ptolemaic Kingdom since its first king. Rome was careful about seizing new provinces. It did not usually annex new lands without the assurance that political consequences, if any, would be minimal. They were right. Ptolemy XII let the province go. He was in no position to fight Rome.

Ptolemy XII[46]

In 65 BCE, the Roman censor Crassus recommended annexing Egypt itself. "When Ptolemy X died, he left Egypt to Rome in his will!"

Julius Caesar, a rising political star, supported Crassus.

Nevertheless, the senators shot it down: "Crassus! You know it was only valid if he had no surviving sons. Ptolemy XI Alexander was his son! Furthermore, no one here in Rome has ever seen that will. It's probably just a rumor. At any rate, trying to take Egypt at this point is too risky."

Nevertheless, Ptolemy XII began bribing the Roman senators to ensure their vote against attacking Egypt. Meanwhile, General Pompey had been sweeping through Anatolia and Syria, making them part of Rome's empire. His next target was Judea. Ptolemy XII sent a gold crown to Pompey and paid for eight thousand cavalry to use in his war against his neighbor. He did not want to be Pompey's next target.

Pompey, Caesar, and Crassus formed the First Triumvirate, which got Caesar elected as Rome's consul. Ptolemy XII traveled to Rome to cement recognition from Rome of his kingship. He bribed Caesar and Pompey with six thousand talents (Egypt's annual revenue) and won the title *socius et amicus* (ally and friend) by the Senate's decree. Rome and Egypt made a formal alliance.

Most of Egypt disapproved of the bribery scheme. For one thing, it broke Egypt's bank, leading to crushing taxes. Secondly, it was embarrassing that Egypt was groveling before Rome. Even worse, the Romans ignored the alliance when they snatched Cyprus the following year. Even when Ptolemy XII's brother, the governor of Cyprus, committed suicide, Ptolemy XII did nothing.

The Alexandrians poured into the streets in protest, calling for Ptolemy XII's expulsion from Egypt. Even before the Cyprus debacle, the priesthood and military had grown to loathe Ptolemy XII. The king fled to Rome in 58 BCE, leaving most of his family behind. The Alexandrians placed his oldest daughter, Berenice IV, on the throne. Cleopatra IV, either another wife or daughter, ruled with her. His second daughter, Cleopatra VII, "the" Cleopatra, went with him to Rome.

Most senators turned their backs on Ptolemy XII in Rome despite him being an ally. However, Pompey took him and Cleopatra VII into his villa and interceded for him with the Senate. He finally persuaded the Senate to restore Ptolemy XII to the throne. Nevertheless, they had a peculiar problem. An ancient oracle said that if Rome got involved in attacking Egypt because an Egyptian pharaoh asked for help, disaster would come down on Rome.

In Egypt, Berenice IV continued ruling, but Cleopatra VI either died or withdrew from politics. Berenice's position was tenuous, as she had no husband, which the Alexandrians felt was improper. They found her a husband, Archelaus, from the house of Mithridates. However, he was only her husband, not co-ruler.

In Rome, Ptolemy XII borrowed money heavily to fund his restoration to Egypt. He paid ten thousand talents to Aulus Gabinius, a Roman general and proconsul of Syria, to attack Egypt. Since Archelaus's "pirate" fleets had allegedly been stealing grain shipments to

Syria, the feeling was that now, war was justified. It was not so much about restoring the old king as removing the man behind the piracy.

Gabinius successfully attacked Egypt, killed Archelaus, and restored Ptolemy XII to the throne in 55 BCE. The twists and turns of politics sometimes meant that friends ended up fighting each other. Archelaus's friend, Mark Antony, led Gabinius's cavalry in the invasion yet gave Archelaus a proper burial.

The Alexandrians were still rioting, so Gabinius enslaved the ringleaders. Ptolemy XII wasted no time getting revenge on his enemies. He even killed his daughter, Berenice IV, who had ruled Egypt in his absence. He replaced the city's leaders with unsuitable and unrefined men.

Now, Ptolemy XII had a new problem. He had borrowed a fortune from Rome's creditors, and they wanted repayment. Emptying Egypt's treasury would not be enough. Ptolemy XII appointed Rabirius Postumus, a Roman banker, to be Egypt's new treasurer. Postumus confiscated the wealth of the Alexandrians who opposed Ptolemy XII to pay back the debt. Then, he imposed more taxes. This riled up the Alexandrians again, and Postumus fled to Rome.

Not everyone in Rome got their money back. When Julius Caesar sailed into Alexandria in 48 BCE, he presented an outstanding debt of 17,500,000 denarii, demanding the heirs of Ptolemy Aulete pay 10,000,000, possibly Caesar's share of the loan.[i]

Ptolemy XII died in 51 BCE. His will stated that his son Ptolemy XIII and his daughter Cleopatra VII should get married and be the next rulers. He sent a copy of his will to Rome, and it ended up in Pompey's hands. Rome was in the midst of a civil war, leaving Egypt to its own devices for the time being.

Cleopatra VII and Ptolemy XIII Fight for Power

Ptolemy XIII and Cleopatra VII married immediately. The bride was eighteen, but the groom was only eleven. Cleopatra ruled in her own right, and the eunuch Pothinus acted as Ptolemy's regent. The couple's relationship quickly turned sour as each vied for total control. Cleopatra

---

[i] Siani-Davies, "Ptolemy XII Auletes," 31.

was getting the upper hand. Documents and coins only represented Cleopatra, not Ptolemy. By 48 BCE, a civil war erupted between brother and sister. Ptolemy was winning, so Cleopatra fled to Syria and recruited an army to fight her brother.

At this point, Pompey arrived in Egypt. Once close friends and co-conspirators, Pompey and Julius Caesar had fallen out and were now bitter rivals. Caesar was chasing Pompey down, intent on becoming Rome's sole ruler. Ptolemy XIII welcomed Pompey to Egypt, feigning friendship. Nevertheless, he quickly ordered the great general's murder. Ptolemy thought he had a better chance of allying with Julius Caesar than Pompey. Caesar sailed into Egypt shortly after, and Ptolemy XIII greeted him with Pompey's head. It did not have the effect he'd hoped.

"Where's the rest of his body? Find it! Give him a proper Roman burial," Caesar barked. He wept at the funeral of his one-time friend, vowing to avenge his death.

Ptolemy XIII escaped, but Caesar killed the eunuch Pothinus and the two men who had stabbed Pompey. Caesar was now Rome's dictator, and Cleopatra VII, who had just arrived back in Egypt, wanted him on her side. She used her feminine wiles to make that happen. Caesar and Cleopatra became lovers and joined their armies against Ptolemy XIII.

From December 48 to February 47 BCE, the two forces clashed. Sadly, the Library of Alexandria caught fire in the fighting. Caesar and Cleopatra won, and while escaping, Ptolemy drowned in the Nile. Caesar placed Cleopatra back on Egypt's throne with her younger brother, twelve-year-old Ptolemy XIV, as her co-regent and new husband. Rather than rushing back to Rome, Caesar enjoyed two months with Cleopatra, and she conceived their child, Caesarion.

Caesar returned to Rome, where he ruled until 44 BCE as consul and dictator. Although they liked his reforms, the Senate feared he would return Rome to a monarchy. As he entered the Senate on March 15, 44 BCE, the senators surrounded him and stabbed him to death. Cleopatra was staying at Caesar's villa in Italy with her little son, Caesarion. She immediately left for Egypt. Several months later, when he was three years old, she declared Caesarion her co-ruler.

Cleopatra VII and Caesarion[47]

Mark Antony was Rome's consul and Caesar's right-hand man at the time. Holding Caesar's bloody toga, he presided over Caesar's funeral. The conspirators who had murdered Caesar had fled, leaving Antony as Rome's de facto leader. However, Caesar's will shook things up. He named his nephew, Octavian, as his heir. Antony expected to step into Caesar's shoes, but now he had a nineteen-year-old contender. The Romans liked young Octavian better. He eventually became Rome's next consul and, as Caesar Augustus, ruled Rome for the rest of his life.

As part of a deal with Octavian, Antony became the ruler of all Rome's eastern provinces. In 41 BCE, while in Tarsus, Anatolia, Antony asked Cleopatra to meet with him. Egypt was still technically independent, and he wanted to work out an alliance with Rome. Cleopatra arrived in style, sailing into Tarsus in a splendid boat with purple sails and silver oars. The sound of flutes and lyres drifted through the air as little boys dressed as Cupids fanned their queen, who was dressed as Aphrodite.

Antony instantly fell under her sway and sailed back to Alexandria with her. The following year, she gave birth to twins, Cleopatra Selene and Alexander Helios. Eventually, Antony's jealous wife, Fulvia, Rome's most powerful woman, began stirring up trouble in Italy. Antony left Egypt to sort things out. Fulvia died suddenly and suspiciously, and weeks later, Antony married Octavian's sister, Octavia.

Of course, it was just a political marriage. Antony got annoyed when Octavian did not send him enough troops for his Parthian expedition. He returned to his lover, Cleopatra, who had plenty of soldiers to help him. In 36 BCE, Cleopatra had another son with him, Ptolemy Philadelphus.

In Rome, Octavian found Antony's secret will and discovered Antony planned to give some of Rome's provinces to his sons with Cleopatra. In the will, he called Cleopatra his "queen" and gave instructions to bury him with her in Alexandria.

What alarmed Octavian the most was that Antony declared that Caesarion was Caesar's biological son and heir. Octavian was only Caesar's "son" by adoption. Caesarion presented a grave threat to Octavian's inheritance and political ambitions. Octavian had the Senate declare war on Cleopatra, yet a third of the Senate went over to Antony's side.

The Battle of Actium

In 31 BCE, the naval Battle of Actium was the decisive showdown. Antony and Cleopatra fought against Octavian and his naval commander, Agrippa. The battle occurred in the Ionian Sea off Actium on Greece's western coast. Octavian's army had 3,000 archers, 80,000 troops, and 12,000 cavalry. His navy had 400 lightweight and easily maneuverable ships carrying catapults. The catapults launched harpoons, which hooked the Egyptian ships, enabling the Romans to pull them close and board.

The Egyptians had 480 ships, 70,000 infantry, and 12,000 cavalry. However, the Egyptian ships were heavier and more challenging to maneuver, although they made good platforms for archers. Several kings fought with Antony, including those from Libya, Cilicia, and Thrace. Other kings sent armies to help, including King Herod the Jew and King Malchus of Arabia.[i]

---

[i] Plutarch, *Plutarch's Lives*, trans. Bernadotte Perrin (Harvard University Press, 1920), chap. 6, https://www.perseus.tufts.edu/hopper/text?doc=Perseus%3Atext%3A2008.01.0007%3Achapter%3D6.

A strait that led into the Ambracian Gulf divided the opposing land forces, so they did not engage. Plutarch said that Antony's infantry and cavalry were superior to Octavian's, so Octavian purposefully did not fight him on land. Antony did not press the matter because Cleopatra insisted on a sea battle. Even so, she did not position her ships in the most strategic places to win. Instead, she had them where they could most easily escape if the battle did not go well.

When the battle began, the plan was for Antony's ships *not* to go into the open sea but to stay in the gulf and the narrows. They could launch arrows and other projectiles without being surrounded by the Roman's smaller and faster ships. However, some of his ship captains thought their size made them unapproachable. They got irritated by the delay and sailed out into open water, much to Octavian's glee. His smaller vessels had the speed and agility to surround them and get close. However, they couldn't use the harpoons to catch the ships and board. The Egyptian ships were too high, and their hulls were too hard.

Battle of Actium by Laureys a Castro[48]

Although neither side had the upper hand in the sea battle, Cleopatra suddenly gathered her sixty ships and sailed south, away from the battle. The Romans dropped their jaws in surprise. When Antony saw her leaving, he sailed after her with forty ships. The rest of his vessels were tangled with the Romans and could not leave. Antony sent word to his land forces, "Retreat! Cross over to Anatolia. Keep going to Syria."

After Cleopatra and Antony abandoned the battle, their remaining ships fought fiercely but were overwhelmingly outnumbered. A squall blew in high waves that shattered some vessels. Five thousand troops defending Egypt died, and Caesar captured three hundred ships. Meanwhile, Antony's infantry and cavalry kept waiting for him to arrive, even though he had messaged them to leave immediately. Finally, after a week, they surrendered to Rome.

The Final Downfall

Back in Egypt, Cleopatra paced back and forth, trying to make plans. Antony sat staring into space, depressed and drinking heavily. In July of 30 BCE, Octavian arrived, spurring Antony into action. At first, Antony was winning the battle, but then his troops began deserting, realizing that resistance was futile. Antony fell on his sword, dying in Cleopatra's embrace. Cleopatra killed herself, probably by poison or snakebite, on August 30, 30 BCE. Octavian buried them together in Alexandria. He gave Cleopatra's younger children to his sister to raise, yet killed her oldest son, seventeen-year-old Caesarion—the last pharaoh of Ptolemaic Egypt. Egypt was now a Roman province.

Did the Romans follow the Ptolemaic administration model in Egypt?

The Ptolemies and Romans had similar ways of doing government. Both had a strong central government and a hierarchy of administrators. Both governments followed strict procedures. Egypt had been divided into nomes (territories) from ancient times. The Persians adopted this system, followed by the Ptolemies and then Rome. The Romans did not make many changes in Egypt. They replaced a few Greek administrators with Romans but kept many Greeks in office. They put the Roman legal system into play. The Ptolemies already had a highly organized taxation system, which the Romans adopted. Greek continued to be the administrative language, with Latin added in.

Chapter 9: Legacy of the Ptolemaic Kingdom Beyond Egypt

The Ptolemaic Kingdom left a profound legacy on history and culture. Its enduring influence spread far beyond its heartland, Egypt. The world owes a debt to the stunning breakthroughs of the mathematicians and scientists at Alexandria's Library. Alexandria's poets, tragedians, and other literary giants lifted the world to new creative heights. As great minds came together and exchanged ideas, they sparked astonishing strides in intellectual growth.

Mathematics, Science, and Astronomy

Euclid of Alexandria made mind-blowing progress in geometry and logic in Ptolemy I's reign. He wrote a mathematical treatise called *The Elements*. It contained thirteen books on geometry, number theory, and mathematical proofs, including the work of earlier mathematicians. Euclid took earlier theories and developed them further, providing solid proofs. He explained parallel postulates, the Pythagorean theorem, and Euclidian geometry. *The Elements* is the world's oldest mathematical collection that still exists today.

Aristarchus of Samos moved to Alexandria to study natural science under Strato of Lampsacus. Aristarchus specialized in astronomy. He was the first to suggest that the Earth traveled with other planets around the sun each year. Most people believed that the Earth was the center of the universe, but Aristarchus said that the sun was the center. However, he could not convince other scholars. Eighteen centuries later, Nicolaus Copernicus presented the idea again, and it finally caught on. Aristarchus also taught that the Earth turned on an axis each day and that the stars were far-away suns.

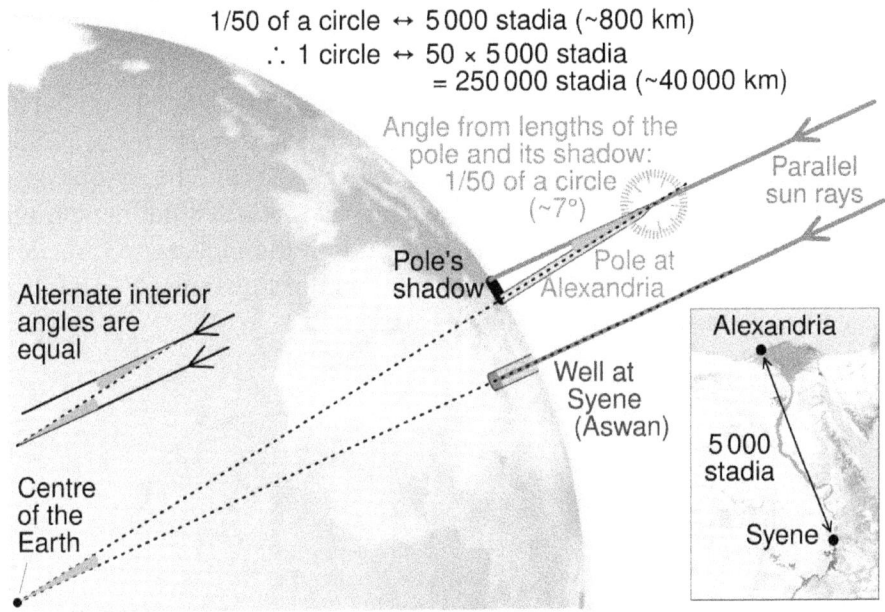

How Eratosthenes estimated the Earth's circumference[49]

By this time, Greek philosophers were realizing that the Earth was not flat but a sphere. Eratosthenes, head of the Library of Alexandria in Ptolemy II's reign, figured out the Earth's circumference. In Alexandria, Eratosthenes went outside at noon on June 21 and stuck a stick in the ground. He noted a shadow with a seven-degree angle. Meanwhile, he had sent a man to Syene, down the Nile from Alexandria. His assistant measured the distance between the cities and the shadow cast by a stick in the ground in Syene at noon on June 21. Comparing these measurements, Eratosthenes calculated that the Earth's circumference was 250,000 stadia (28,000 miles). He was incredibly close! Today's calculations place the distance around the Earth at 24,901 miles.

As a teen, Archimedes of Syracuse traveled from Sicily to study at the Library of Alexandria, where he rubbed shoulders with Eratosthenes. Archimedes would get so engrossed in mathematical calculations that he forgot to eat. After his studies, he returned to Sicily but maintained a lively correspondence with Alexandria's scholars. He was ancient history's greatest mathematician, making staggering advances in calculus and geometry.

Archimedes used geometry to estimate square roots and figured out a theoretical calculation of pi (π) – the ratio of circumference to diameter in a circle. By drawing polygons inside a circle, he came up with an approximation between 3.14285 and 3.14084. Today's mathematicians put pi's first ten digits as 3.1415926535.

Another brainchild of Archimedes was the "Law of the Lever." He discovered that even a small person could lift a heavy weight using a rock and a long stick—something like a seesaw. The closer the heavy object is to the fulcrum or center of the seesaw, the easier it is for the person on the other end to push down on the stick and lift the object. Archimedes claimed anyone could apply this principle to lifting anything: "Give me a place to stand, and I shall move the earth!"

Archimedes's Law of the Lever[50]

Archimedes' interest in moving heavy objects also led to his invention of the first compound pulley, which he used to move a ship. He discovered that a sphere's volume is two-thirds the volume of a cylinder surrounding it. (Think about a ball fitted inside a can that has both ends open.) Archimedes was so proud of this calculation that he asked for it to be inscribed on his tomb (and it was).

Poets and Tragedians

Greek poets and drama writers clustered at the Library of Alexandria. In Ptolemy II's reign, seven of the most brilliant writers formed the "Alexandrian Pleiad." The name came from the Pleiades constellation, which has seven stars the human eye can see. The Alexandrian Pleiad included Philiscus of Corcyra. As a priest of Dionysus, Philiscus marched in Ptolemy II's coronation procession. He wrote forty-two tragic dramas.

Another Pleiad writer was Lycophron, who organized the comedy section of the Library of Alexandria. He wrote both comedies and tragedies. Lycophron probably wrote *Alexandra*, in which the Trojan priestess Cassandra prophesies that the Trojan descendants (Romans) would rule the earth and sea.

A third Pleiad author was Sositheus, who wrote satyr plays combining comedy and tragedy. His play *Daphnis* is the tale of Daphnis, the shepherd, searching for his true love. He encountered Lityerses, the "Reaper of Men," who forced him into a competition. Who could reap the fastest? The loser would die! The hero Heracles came to the shepherd's rescue and killed Lityerses. Theocritus, another Pleiad poet at Alexandria, picked up Daphnis's story. Unfortunately, the shepherd died of lovesickness, taunted by Aphrodite, the goddess of love: "You tried to 'bend' love, but instead, it bent you."

Alexander Aetolus was another member of the Pleiad. He assisted in the mammoth task of organizing and revising the classical Greek literature collection at the Library of Alexandria. He was a poet with a range of styles but was mainly known for his tragedies. One of his plays was the *Astragalistai*, meaning "Knucklebone-players." It tells the story of the child Patroklos, who later became a hero of the Trojan War. Patroklos argued with his playmate Clysonymus over a game of dice, accidentally killed him, and was exiled.

Philosophy

The philosopher Strato (Straton) taught Ptolemy II and Aristarchus. He focused on natural science, taking the teachings of his mentor Aristotle to the next level. Aristotle believed in the eternal, unchanging, perfect "unmoved mover." However, Strato did not believe in a creator god. Instead, he thought the divine yet unconscious force of nature caused creation.

Strato believed natural law kept the universe running without the gods doing anything. He believed that hot and cold temperatures, especially heat, made things happen. He said the stars were made from "fiery stuff" and had to obey the laws of gravity like everything else. Strato believed the moon and some "stars" (planets) reflected the sun's light. Strato taught that a child was conceived by "γονή" (semen or reproductive material) from both its mother and father. A child's gender was determined by which parent had the most potent "semen."

Unlike Strato, most Greeks and Egyptians in Ptolemaic Egypt believed in many gods. They thought these deities controlled the universe and intervened in the lives of humans. However, as mentioned, up to a quarter of Alexandria's population were Jews who believed in only one god. Most Ptolemaic rulers gave religious freedom to the Jews. The grateful Jews even dedicated synagogues to the Ptolemaic kings.

Philo of Alexandria[51]

Aristobulus of Alexandria was a Jewish philosopher in the reign of Ptolemy VI. He fused Judaism and Hellenism. His life mission was to drive home his belief that Judaism influenced Greek thought, even as far back as Homer and Hesiod. Philo of Alexandria was a Jewish philosopher in the final days of Ptolemaic rule. He taught that true existence only happens when a person recognizes he or she is nothing without God, the source of *logos* (reason).

Conclusion

A fascinating aspect of the Ptolemaic Kingdom was that the Greeks invaded and liberated Egypt simultaneously. The Egyptians had suffered horrifically under the harsh Persian rule. Undoubtedly, the Egyptians would have preferred self-rule, but that was not an option. If they had to be ruled by foreigners, they preferred Greek administration over Persian.

The only Persian ruler they liked was the third: Darius I. He improved Egypt's agriculture through irrigation projects and enhanced trade by completing a canal to the Red Sea. He also rebuilt their temples and honored their priests. After Darius, Persian rule mainly went downhill for Egypt. The Persians took Egypt's best and brightest—their skilled artisans, architects, and doctors—to Persia. They placed crushing taxes on the remaining Egyptians and disrespected their temples. By contrast, the Greeks and Egyptians had enjoyed a primarily friendly and beneficial relationship for over a millennia. They traded, shared culture, and defended each other against common enemies.

Although the Greeks held the political reins, they did not consider themselves more enlightened or cultured. They valued and embraced aspects of Egyptian culture while maintaining their own traditions. They initiated new cults revolving around the Ptolemaic kings, but even that was an Egyptian tradition. They translated Egyptian histories, medical books, and literature into Greek. The Ptolemies were champions of compromise and cultural blending.

The lively Ptolemaic economy benefited all of Egypt, both Greeks and Egyptians. With Alexandria as a hub, trade around the Mediterranean skyrocketed. New crops and improved irrigation led to abundant food to feed the rapidly doubling population and sell to foreign countries. The Ptolemaic Kingdom also initiated a cultural revival that took the world by storm. The Library of Alexandria drew razor-sharp scholars from around the ancient world who shared ideas and developed thrilling new ones.

What if the Ptolemaic Kingdom never ruled Egypt? What would the world have lacked? One can only imagine the stimulating cultural and economic growth the Mediterranean region would have missed without Ptolemaic rule! The astounding breakthroughs achieved by the scholars at the Library of Alexandria would not have happened. How many centuries would the world have needed to wait for such incredible advances in science and mathematics?

Furthermore, while his fellow Diadochi were grabbing up as many provinces as possible, Ptolemy I saw Egypt as a desirable land in and of itself. He envisioned what Egypt could be, with its water highways reaching most of the known world. He put his vision into play, and Alexandria became the jewel of Alexander's one-time empire.

Hundreds of years later, Egypt persisted as a major player in the Roman Empire. It became Rome's primary source of grain. Alexandria continued as a trade center and cultural hub. Today, with a population of five million, it is the largest city on the Mediterranean Sea. The "Bride of the Mediterranean" still reigns as a major port and industrial center.

Here's another book by Enthralling History that you might like

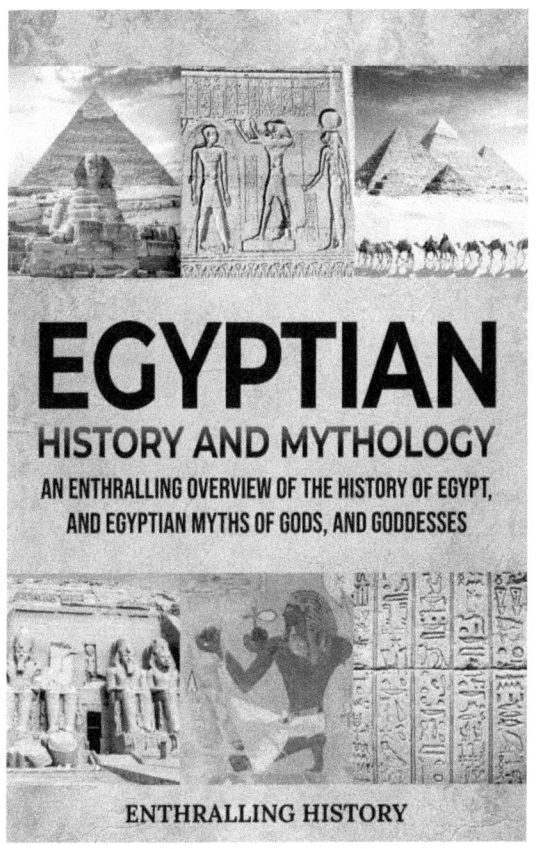

Free limited time bonus

Stop for a moment. We have a free bonus set up for you. The problem is this: we forget 90% of everything that we read after 7 days. Crazy fact, right? Here's the solution: we've created a printable, 1-page pdf summary for this book that you're reading now. All you have to do to get your free pdf summary is to go to the following website: https://livetolearn.lpages.co/enthrallinghistory/

Or, Scan the QR code!

Once you do, it will be intuitive. Enjoy, and thank you!

Bibliography

Africanus, Sextus Julius. "The king lists of Africanus." Pharoah.se. Accessed November 27, 2024. https://pharaoh.se/africanus-king-list.

Arrian. "Alexander the Great." In *The Anabasis and the Indica*. Translated by Martin Hammond. Oxford University Press, 2013.

Bennett, Bob and Mike Roberts. *The Wars of Alexander's Successors, 323-281 BC Volume 1: Commanders and Campaigns*. Pen & Sword Military, 2013.

Bennett, Bob and Mike Roberts. *The Wars of Alexander's Successors 323-281 BC Volume 2: Battles and Tactics*. Pen & Sword Military, 2009.

Bevan, E. R. *The House of Ptolemy*. Methuen Publishing, 1927. https://penelope.uchicago.edu/Thayer/E/Gazetteer/Places/Africa/Egypt/_Texts/BEVHOP/6*.html.

Buraselis, Kostas. "Ptolemaic Grain, Seaways and Power." In *The Ptolemies, the Sea and the Nile: Studies in Waterborne Power*, edited by Kostas Buraselis, Mary Stefanou, and Dorothy J. Thompson. Cambridge University Press, 2013.

Clayman, Dee L. *Berenice II and the Golden Age of Ptolemaic Egypt (Women in Antiquity)*. Oxford University Press, 2014.

De la Bedoyere, Guy. *The Fall of Egypt and the Rise of Rome: A History of the Ptolemies*. Yale University Press, 2024.

Dillon, John, and Lloyd P. Gerson. *Neoplatonic Philosophy: Introductory Readings*. Hackett Publishing Company, 2004.

Diodorus, Siculus. *Library of History*. Translated by C. Bradford Welles. Harvard University Press, 1963.

Eusebius. *The Egyptian Chronicle*. Translated by Robert Bedrosian. Accessed November 27, 2024. http://www.attalus.org/armenian/euseb.html.

Fisher-Bovet, Christelle. *Army and Society in Ptolemaic Egypt (Armies of the Ancient World)*. Cambridge University Press, 2014.

Flavius, Josephus. *The Antiquities of the Jews*. Translated by William Whiston. Project Gutenberg eBook, October 1, 2001.
https://www.gutenberg.org/cache/epub/2848/pg2848-images.html.

Grainger, John D. *The Ptolemies, Rise of a Dynasty: Ptolemaic Egypt 330-246 BC*. Pen & Sword Books, 2022.

Hauben, Hans. "Review of 'Army and Society in Ptolemaic Egypt: From Invasion to Integration' by Christelle Fischer-Bovet," *The Bulletin of the American Society of Papyrologists* 53 (2016): 395-409.
http://www.jstor.org/stable/44968458.

Herodotus, *The Histories*. Translated by George Rawlinson. Dutton & Co, 1862. http://classics.mit.edu/Herodotus/history.html.

Hölbl, Günther. *A History of the Ptolemaic Empire*. Translated by Tina Saavedra. Routledge, 2000.

Homer. *The Odyssey*. Translated by Samuel Butler. Internet Classics Archive. Accessed November 27, 2024. http://classics.mit.edu/Homer/odyssey.html.

Johstono, Paul A. *The Army of Ptolemaic Egypt 323-204 BC: An Institutional and Operational History*. Pen & Sword Military, 2020.

Justinus. *Epitome of Pompeius Trogus' Philippic Histories*. Translated by J. S. Watson, 1853. https://www.attalus.org/translate/justin4.html#26.1.

Manning, J. G. *Land and Power in Ptolemaic Egypt*. Cambridge University Press, 2007.

Manning, J. G., F. Ludlow, A.R. Stine, W. Boos, M. Sigl, and J. R. Marlon. "Volcanic Suppression of Nile Summer Flooding Triggers Revolt and Constrains Interstate Conflict in Ancient Egypt." *Nature Communications* 8, no. 900 (2017). https://doi.org/10.1038/s41467-017-00957-y.

Marr J. S., and C. H. Calisher. "Alexander the Great and West Nile Virus Encephalitis." *Emerging Infectious Diseases*, 9, no. 12 (December 2003):1599-603. https://doi.org10.3201/eid0912.030288 . PMID: 14725285; PMCID: PMC3034319.

Matyszak, Philip. *Greece Against Rome: The Fall of the Hellenistic Kingdoms 250-31 BC*. Pen & Sword Military, 2020.

Plutarch. "Moralia." *Isis and Osiris*. Loeb Classical Library, 1936.
https://penelope.uchicago.edu/Thayer/e/roman/texts/plutarch/moralia/isis_and_osiris*/b.html.

Plutarch. *Plutarch's Lives*. Translated by Bernadotte Perrin. Harvard University Press, 1920.
https://www.perseus.tufts.edu/hopper/text?doc=Perseus%3Atext%3A2008.01.0007%3Achapter%3D61.

Plutarch. *The Life of Alexander the Great.* Translated by John Dryden. Modern Library Paperback Edition, 2004.

Polyaenus. *Stratagems: Book Seven.* Translated by R. Shepherd, 1793. http://www.attalus.org/translate/polyaenus7.html.

Polybius, *The Histories.* Book V. Loeb Classical Library Edition, 1923. https://penelope.uchicago.edu/Thayer/E/Roman/Texts/Polybius/5*.html.

Siani-Davies, Mary. "Ptolemy XII Auletes and the Romans." *Historia: Zeitschrift Für Alte Geschichte* 46, no. 3 (1997): 306–40. http://www.jstor.org/stable/4436474.

The Complete Tanakh: The Jewish Bible with a Modern English Translation and Rashi's Commentary. Accessed November 27, 2024. https://www.chabad.org/library/bible_cdo/aid/63255/jewish/The-Bible-with-Rashi.htm.

The Letter of Aristeas to Philocrates. Translated by R. H. Charles, 1913. https://www.attalus.org/translate/aristeas1.html.

Theocritus. *The Project Gutenberg eBook of Theocritus.* Accessed November 27, 2024. https://www.gutenberg.org/files/11533/11533-h/11533-h.htm#IDYLL_XIV.

Von Reden, S. *Money in Ptolemaic Egypt.* Cambridge University Press, 2010.

Worthington, Ian. *By the Spear: Philip II, Alexander the Great, and the Rise and Fall of the Macedonian Empire (Ancient Warfare and Civilization).* Oxford University Press, 2016.

Zielinski, Sarah. "After 2,000 Years, Ptolemy's War Elephants are Revealed." *Science News: Archaeology,* January 21, 2014. https://www.sciencenews.org/blog/wild-things/after-2000-years-ptolemys-war-elephants-are-revealed.

Image Sources

[1] *Zoomed in, labels added. Source: Joe Roe, CC BY-SA 4.0 <https://creativecommons.org/licenses/by-sa/4.0>, via Wikimedia Commons: https://commons.wikimedia.org/wiki/File:Middle_East_topographic_map.png*

[2] *Gunawan Kartapranata, CC BY-SA 3.0 <https://creativecommons.org/licenses/by-sa/3.0>, via Wikimedia Commons: https://commons.wikimedia.org/wiki/File:Bastet.svg*

[3] *https://commons.wikimedia.org/wiki/File:Cambyses_II_capturing_Psamtik_III.png*

[4] *https://commons.wikimedia.org/wiki/File:Makedonische_phalanx.png*

[5] *https://commons.wikimedia.org/wiki/File:Meister_der_Alexanderschlacht_003.jpg*

[6] *https://commons.wikimedia.org/wiki/File:Alexander_and_Bucephalus_-_Battle_of_Issus_mosaic_-_Museo_Archeologico_Nazionale_-_Naples_BW.jpg*

[7] *https://commons.wikimedia.org/wiki/File:Ptolemy_I_Soter_Louvre_Ma849.jpg*

[8] *Stella, CC BY-SA 4.0 <https://creativecommons.org/licenses/by-sa/4.0>, via Wikimedia Commons: https://commons.wikimedia.org/wiki/File:Ptolemy_I_as_Pharaoh_of_Egypt.jpg*

[9] *Photo zoomed in, labels highlighted. Source: Jeff Dahl, CC BY-SA 4.0 <https://creativecommons.org/licenses/by-sa/4.0>, via Wikimedia Commons: https://commons.wikimedia.org/wiki/File:Ancient_Egypt_map-en.svg*

[10] *Gnauth, Adolf, CC BY-SA 2.5 <https://creativecommons.org/licenses/by-sa/2.5>, via Wikimedia Commons: https://commons.wikimedia.org/wiki/File:Ancient_Alexandria_(1878)_-_TIMEA.jpg*

[11] *drawing by Kaidor, English text by Ashaio, CC BY-SA 3.0 <https://creativecommons.org/licenses/by-sa/3.0>, via Wikimedia Commons: https://commons.wikimedia.org/wiki/File:Ptolemaic_Alexandria_-_en.svg*

[12] *Віщун, CC BY-SA 4.0 <https://creativecommons.org/licenses/by-sa/4.0>, via Wikimedia Commons https://commons.wikimedia.org/wiki/File:Pharos_of_Alexandria,_reconstruction_2021.jpg*

[13] *Epiphanesnikophoros, CC BY-SA 4.0 <https://creativecommons.org/licenses/by-sa/4.0>, via Wikimedia Commons: https://commons.wikimedia.org/wiki/File:Ptolemaic_Kingdom_Ptolemy_I_Soter.jpg*

[14] *Massimo Finizio, CC BY-SA 2.0 via Wikimedia Commons: https://commons.wikimedia.org/wiki/File:Seleuco_I_Nicatore.JPG*

[15] *Scan by NYPL, CC BY-SA 4.0 <https://creativecommons.org/licenses/by-sa/4.0>, via Wikimedia Commons: https://commons.wikimedia.org/wiki/File:Ptolemy_(II)_Philadelphos.jpg*

[16] *Sailko, CC BY-SA 3.0 <https://creativecommons.org/licenses/by-sa/3.0>, via Wikimedia Commons: https://commons.wikimedia.org/wiki/File:Cammeo_gonzaga_con_doppio_ritratto_di_tolomeo_II_e_arsinoe_II,_III_sec._ac._(alessandria),_da_hermitage.jpg*

[17] *Miguel Hermoso Cuesta, CC BY-SA 3.0 <https://creativecommons.org/licenses/by-sa/3.0>, via Wikimedia Commons: https://commons.wikimedia.org/wiki/File:Ptolomeo_III.JPG*

[18] *[1], CC BY-SA 4.0 <https://creativecommons.org/licenses/by-sa/4.0>, via Wikimedia Commons: https://commons.wikimedia.org/wiki/File:Ptolemaius_III_Euergetes_a_Berenice_II-Propylon_Khonsu_Tempes.png*

[19] *Sailko, CC BY 3.0 <https://creativecommons.org/licenses/by/3.0>, via Wikimedia Commons: https://commons.wikimedia.org/wiki/File:Egitto_tolemaico,_berenice_II,_octodracma_di_efeso,_246-222_ac_ca.JPG*

[20] *Classical Numismatic Group, Inc. http://www.cngcoins.com, CC BY-SA 3.0 <http://creativecommons.org/licenses/by-sa/3.0 >, via Wikimedia Commons: https://commons.wikimedia.org/wiki/File:Silver_tetradrachm,_Ptolemy_IV_Philopator,_221-205_BC.jpg*

[21] *Nicolaes Witsen, Public domain, via Wikimedia Commons: https://commons.wikimedia.org/wiki/File:Thalamegos_Nicolaes_Witsen_1671.jpg*

[22] *ArchaiOptix, CC BY-SA 4.0 <https://creativecommons.org/licenses/by-sa/4.0>, via Wikimedia Commons: https://commons.wikimedia.org/wiki/File:Egypt_-_king_Ptolemaios_V_-_204-203_BC_-_gold_oktadrachm_-_bust_of_Ptolemaios_V_-_cornucopiae_-_Berlin_MK_AM_18203067.jpg*

[23] *https://commons.wikimedia.org/wiki/File:Rosetta_Stone_BW.jpeg*

[24] *Metropolitan Museum of Art, CC0, via Wikimedia Commons: https://commons.wikimedia.org/wiki/File:Faience_Sistrum_Inscribed_with_the_Name_of_Ptolemy_I_MET_DP246588.jpg*

[25] *Photo zoomed in. Hedwig Storch, CC BY-SA 3.0 <https://creativecommons.org/licenses/by-sa/3.0>, via Wikimedia Commons: https://commons.wikimedia.org/wiki/File:Kom_Ombo,_Sobek_0319.JPG*

[26] *https://commons.wikimedia.org/wiki/File:Bust_Serapis_Chiaramonti.jpg*

[27] *https://commons.wikimedia.org/wiki/File:Maler_der_Grabkammer_des_Sennudem_001.jpg*

[28] *Igor Merit Santos, CC BY-SA 4.0 <https://creativecommons.org/licenses/by-sa/4.0>, via Wikimedia Commons:* https://commons.wikimedia.org/wiki/File:The_Great_Library_of_Alexandria,_O._Von_Corven,_19th_century.jpg

[29] *Yair Haklai, CC BY-SA 4.0 <https://creativecommons.org/licenses/by-sa/4.0>, via Wikimedia Commons:* https://commons.wikimedia.org/wiki/File:Bust_of_Demetrius_Phalereus_at_Kunsthistorisches_Museum.jpg

[30] https://commons.wikimedia.org/wiki/File:Ptolem%C3%A4er-_Ptolemaios_III._-_M%C3%BCnzkabinett,_Berlin_-_5531438.jpg

[31] *Ptolemaic Kingdom III-II century BC - ru.svg: Kaidor (talk · contribs)derivative work: rowanwindwhistler (talk)derivative work: Amphipolis, CC BY-SA 4.0 <https://creativecommons.org/licenses/by-sa/4.0>, via Wikimedia Commons:* https://commons.wikimedia.org/wiki/File:Ptolemaic_Kingdom_III-II_century_BC_-_en.svg

[32] https://commons.wikimedia.org/wiki/File:The_Ptolemy_Philophator%27s_%22forty%22_ship,_from_Man_upon_the_sea_-_or,_a_history_of_maritime_adventure,_exploration,_and_discovery,_from_the_earliest_ages_to_the_present_time_(1858)_(14596783329).jpg

[33] *Photo zoomed in.* https://commons.wikimedia.org/wiki/File:Egyptian_harvest.jpg

[34] *Sailko, CC BY 3.0 <https://creativecommons.org/licenses/by/3.0>, via Wikimedia Commons:* https://commons.wikimedia.org/wiki/File:Applique_in_faience_per_tempietti_in_legno,_periodo_tolemaico,_falco_01.JPG

[35] *Photo zoomed in.* https://commons.wikimedia.org/wiki/File:NileMosaicOfPalestrinaSoldiers.jpg#file:

[36] *Khruner, CC BY-SA 4.0 <https://creativecommons.org/licenses/by-sa/4.0>, via Wikimedia Commons:* https://commons.wikimedia.org/wiki/File:Machimoi_by_Khruner.jpg

[37] https://commons.wikimedia.org/wiki/File:Ballista_bw.png

[38] *Photo zoomed in.* https://commons.wikimedia.org/wiki/File:Egypt_and_the_S%C3%BBd%C3%A2n;_handbook_for_travellers_(1914)_(14783598172).jpg

[39] https://commons.wikimedia.org/wiki/File:Peltast.jpg

[40] https://commons.wikimedia.org/wiki/File:Eleazars_exploit.jpg#file

[41] https://commons.wikimedia.org/wiki/File:Ring_with_engraved_portrait_of_Ptolemy_VI_Philometor_(3rd%E2%80%932nd_century_BCE)_-_2009.jpg

[42] *Scan by NYPL, CC BY-SA 4.0 <https://creativecommons.org/licenses/by-sa/4.0>, via Wikimedia Commons:* https://commons.wikimedia.org/wiki/File:Ptolemy_Philometor_and_Cleopatra_II.jpg

[43] *American Numismatic Society, CC0, via Wikimedia Commons:* https://commons.wikimedia.org/wiki/File:Ptolemy_VIII.jpg

[44] https://commons.wikimedia.org/wiki/File:Ptolemy_IX._Soter_II_-_tetradrachma.jpg

[45] *Scan by NYPL, CC BY-SA 4.0 <https://creativecommons.org/licenses/by-sa/4.0>, via Wikimedia Commons:* https://commons.wikimedia.org/wiki/File:Berenice_III.jpg

[46] *Scan by NYPL, CC BY-SA 4.0 <https://creativecommons.org/licenses/by-sa/4.0>, via Wikimedia Commons: https://commons.wikimedia.org/wiki/File:Ptolemy_XII_Dionisos.jpg*

[47] *Photo zoomed in. https://commons.wikimedia.org/wiki/File:Venus_and_Cupid_from_the_House_of_Marcus_Fabius_Rufus_at_Pompeii,_most_likely_a_depiction_of_Cleopatra_VII_(2).jpg*

[48] *https://commons.wikimedia.org/wiki/File:Castro_Battle_of_Actium.jpg*

[49] *cmglee, David Monniaux, jimht at shaw dot ca, CC BY-SA 4.0 <https://creativecommons.org/licenses/by-sa/4.0>, via Wikimedia Commons: https://commons.wikimedia.org/wiki/File:Eratosthenes_measure_of_Earth_circumference.svg*

[50] *Photo zoomed in. ZDF/Terra X/Gruppe 5/ Susanne Utzt, Cristina Trebbi/ Jens Boeck, Dieter Stürmer / Fabian Wienke / Sebastian Martinez/ xkopp, polloq, CC BY 4.0 <https://creativecommons.org/licenses/by/4.0>, via Wikimedia Commons: https://commons.wikimedia.org/wiki/File:Archimedes%27-Lever.png*

[51] *https://commons.wikimedia.org/wiki/File:PhiloThevet.jpg*

www.ingramcontent.com/pod-product-compliance
Lightning Source LLC
Chambersburg PA
CBHW070336010526
44107CB00004B/526